delicious.daily

101+ simply brilliant twists on classic recipes

Recipes by Phoebe Wood

ABC
Books

delicious.daily

Hello

Welcome to *delicious. daily*, a collection of recipes with genius twists to make everyday cooking extraordinary.

At *delicious.* we believe there are few things more wonderful than eating incredible home-cooked food. But when it comes to actually preparing a meal each evening, the pressures of everyday life can certainly take the joy out of the task itself. We created this book to update your weekly recipe rotation, with hacks to make every dish quicker, easier, or more delicious.

Get your week off to an excellent start with make-ahead breakfasts you'll look forward to, then embrace the meat-free-Monday trend with vegetarian meals everyone will enjoy. Master pastry and dough for the easiest-ever pizza, then learn simple tricks that are essential for an easy week. As the weekend draws near, we have one-pot offerings that mean zero hassle, the nourishing goodness of broths, and new ideas to make sure you're never caught off guard by a 'bring-a-plate' invitation again. And let's not forget clever desserts using simply a bowl and spoon. The only fancy thing here is the flavour! This book is your key to make it delicious, every single day.

Contents

Chapter One

Make-ahead breakfast

Doing most of the preparation the night before means you only have to add the finishing touches or reheat in the morning and you're ready to eat. Choose from fruit-filled breads, gluten- and sugar-free granola or a vegie-packed BLAT bowl to get your day off to a nutritious start.

Vintage cheddar & zucchini slice

Serves *8-10*

4 zucchini
5 eggs, lightly beaten
½ cup (80g) pine nuts, toasted, roughly chopped
Finely grated zest of ½ a lemon, plus juice of 1 lemon
1 cup (150g) plain flour
2 tbs finely chopped flat-leaf parsley leaves
200g vintage cheddar, coarsely grated
1 cup (200g) cottage cheese
2 zucchini flowers, petals torn, stems thinly sliced into rounds
Store-bought pesto and micro coriander (optional), to serve

This slice will keep for up to five days in the fridge – simply store without the zucchini flowers and pesto, and add them when ready to serve.

Preheat the oven to 200°C. Grease a 20cm x 30cm lamington pan. Coarsely grate 3 zucchini and squeeze out excess moisture. Place in a bowl with egg, pine nuts, lemon zest, flour, parsley, half the cheddar and the cottage cheese. Season well, then spread into prepared pan.

Using a mandoline, thinly slice remaining zucchini lengthways and arrange over the top in a single layer. Sprinkle with remaining 100g cheddar. Bake for 30 minutes or until cooked through.

Toss zucchini flower petals and stems with lemon juice and season. Scatter over warm zucchini slice and drizzle with pesto. Sprinkle with micro coriander, if using, to serve.

Olive oil granola with rosemary & apricot jam (P 14)

Carrot & haloumi rosti with cauliflower hummus (P 15)

Olive oil granola with rosemary & apricot jam

Free from gluten and refined sugar, this granola is loaded with coconut, nuts and seeds rich in good fats that will help you feel full for longer. It will keep in an airtight container for up to two weeks.

Serves *8*

2 cups (40g) puffed rice
1 cup (50g) coconut flakes
2 tbs black chia seeds
½ cup each sunflower seeds,
   chopped macadamias
   and flaked almonds
1 tsp ground cinnamon
½ cup (125ml) extra virgin olive oil
½ cup (125ml) rice malt syrup
Rosemary leaves and thick
   Greek-style yoghurt, to serve

Cheat's rosemary & apricot jam
200g dried apricots
⅓ cup (80ml) rice malt syrup
2 tsp rosemary leaves,
   finely chopped
2 tsp vanilla bean paste

For the jam, roughly chop half the apricots and place in a saucepan with remaining ingredients, including the whole apricots, and 1 cup (250ml) water. Place over medium heat and cook, stirring occasionally, for 15 minutes or until jammy and caramelised. Remove from heat and cool completely. Jam will keep chilled for up to 3 weeks.

   Meanwhile, to make the granola, preheat the oven to 180°C. Line a baking tray with baking paper. Place all dry ingredients in a large bowl. Add oil and rice malt syrup and, using your hands, combine until mixture is completely coated. Spread over prepared tray and bake for 15 minutes or until golden and toasted. Set aside to cool completely, then break into shards.

   Divide granola among serving bowls, sprinkle with rosemary leaves and serve with yoghurt and jam.

Carrot & haloumi rosti with cauliflower hummus

Serves *6-8*

1 small (about 350g) sweet potato, coarsely grated
1 carrot, coarsely grated
2 eggs, lightly beaten
1 garlic clove, crushed
1 tbs dukkah, plus extra to serve
200g haloumi, coarsely grated
½ cup (75g) plain flour
Finely grated zest and juice of 1 lemon
⅓ cup (80ml) extra virgin olive oil
Sliced green chilli and red vein sorrel leaves, to serve

Cauliflower hummus
400g cauliflower, chopped into small florets
2 tbs extra virgin olive oil
1 tbs tahini
Juice of 1 lemon
1 garlic clove, crushed

This healthy cauliflower hummus is made without pulses and will keep in the fridge for up to five days.

For the cauliflower hummus, preheat the oven to 200°C. Line a baking tray with baking paper. Spread cauliflower in an even layer over the prepared tray and drizzle with oil. Season. Roast for 30 minutes or until tender and golden. Cool slightly, then transfer to a food processor. Add remaining ingredients and whiz until smooth. Season to taste. Chill until needed.

To make the rosti, place sweet potato, carrot, egg, garlic, dukkah, haloumi, flour and lemon zest in a bowl and stir to combine. Season. Heat oil in a large non-stick frypan over medium heat. In 2 batches, add ⅓ cup mixture per rosti to pan, flattening with a spatula. Cook for 5 minutes or until golden, then turn and cook for a further 5 minutes or until crisp and golden.

Divide rosti among serving plates. Top with hummus, extra dukkah, chilli and sorrel. Drizzle with a little lemon juice to serve.

The buttermilk version of this breakfast favourite has oats to sustain you, while sweet potato is the secret ingredient in the spelt loaf that is free from refined sugar. Freeze thick slices and you'll always have an easy brekkie on hand.

Banana, oat & buttermilk spice bread

Serves *8*

4 (about 800g) ripe bananas
150g unsalted butter,
    melted, cooled
1 cup (250g) firmly packed
    brown sugar
3 eggs, lightly beaten
1 tsp vanilla bean paste
2 tsp each ground cinnamon
    and allspice
1 cup (90g) rolled oats
1½ cups (225g) plain flour
1 tsp bicarbonate of soda
½ tsp baking powder
½ cup (125ml) buttermilk
Softened butter and maple syrup
    (optional), to serve

Preheat oven to 160°C. Grease a 1.5L loaf pan and line with baking paper.

Mash 3 bananas in a large bowl. Add melted butter, sugar, egg, vanilla, spices and ¾ cup (65g) oats. Sift in the flour, bicarb and baking powder, then fold in the buttermilk. Stir well to combine. Spoon batter into prepared pan.

Halve the remaining banana lengthways and press into the top of the batter, along with remaining 25g oats. Bake for 55 minutes or until a skewer inserted into the centre comes out clean. Cool in the pan for 30 minutes before turning out onto a wire rack.

Slice and serve with softened butter and maple syrup, if using.

Banana, pear & sweet potato spelt bread

Serves *8*

1 cup cooked, mashed sweet potato
    (from about 400g uncooked)
2 (about 400g) ripe bananas, mashed
150g unsalted butter,
    melted, cooled
¾ cup (180ml) maple syrup,
    plus extra to baste and serve
1½ cups (240g) wholemeal
    spelt flour, sifted
¼ cup (20g) LSA meal (ground
    linseed, sunflower seed, almond)
1 tsp each bicarbonate of soda
    and baking powder
2 eggs, lightly beaten
1½ tsp each ground cinnamon
    and ginger
⅓ cup (80g) sour cream
1 pear, very thinly sliced
Softened butter, to serve

Preheat oven to 180°C. Grease a 1.5L loaf pan and line with baking paper.

Place sweet potato, banana, melted butter, ½ cup (125ml) maple syrup, flour, LSA, bicarb, baking powder, egg, cinnamon, ginger and sour cream in a bowl and stir well to combine. Spoon batter into prepared pan.

Brush pear with remaining 55ml maple syrup and layer over batter. Bake for 1 hour 10 minutes, occasionally basting pear with extra maple, or until a skewer inserted in the centre comes out clean. Cool in the pan for 30 minutes before turning out onto a wire rack.

Slice and serve with softened butter and extra maple syrup.

BLAT quinoa bowl with tomato & bacon ragu (P 20)

Indian breakfast bowl with dill yoghurt and paneer (P 23)
Brown rice nourish bowl with asparagus and sauerkraut (P 21)

BLAT quinoa bowl with tomato & bacon ragu

Having a BLAT for breakfast isn't usually a healthy option, but this fresh and light makeover is full of vegies, protein and fibre.

Serves *4*

1 tbs olive oil
2 garlic cloves, finely chopped
2 spring onions, thinly sliced
1½ cups (300g) quinoa, cooked according to packet instructions
Roasted cherry tomatoes on the vine, avocado, mixed salad leaves, micro cress (optional) and lemon juice, to serve

Tomato & bacon ragu
4 bacon rashers, chopped
3 garlic cloves, finely chopped
4 truss tomatoes, roughly chopped
2 tbs thyme leaves
1 tsp Worcestershire sauce

For the ragu, add bacon to a non-stick frypan and place over medium-low heat. Cook, stirring occasionally, for 10 minutes or until fat begins to render. Add garlic and cook for 2 minutes or until softened. Add tomato, thyme, Worcestershire and ½ cup (125ml) water. Increase heat to medium-high and simmer rapidly for 15 minutes or until tomato is broken down and sauce has reduced. Season and set aside.

Heat oil in a separate frypan over medium heat. Add the garlic and spring onion, and cook, stirring, for 3 minutes or until softened. Add quinoa and stir to coat. Season.

Divide quinoa mixture among serving bowls. Top with ragu, roasted cherry tomatoes, avocado, salad leaves and micro cress, if using. Drizzle with lemon juice just before serving

Brown rice nourish bowl with asparagus and sauerkraut

Low-GI brown rice is a great grain to start the day. This breakfast bowl will work with whatever vegies or salad you have in the fridge.

Serves *4*

1 tbs olive oil
¼ cup (75g) chilli bean paste
   (from Asian food shops)
1 garlic clove, thinly sliced
70g baby spinach leaves
450g packet microwave
   brown rice, heated according
   to packet instructions
2 tbs tamari (gluten-free soy sauce)
   or soy sauce
2 tbs white (shiro) miso
2 tbs organic apple cider vinegar
4 soft-boiled eggs, peeled, halved
Steamed asparagus, thinly sliced
   radish, sauerkraut and micro
   herbs (optional), to serve

Heat the oil in a saucepan over medium-low heat. Add chilli bean paste and garlic, and cook, stirring, for 1 minute or until fragrant. Add spinach and rice, and stir until warmed through.

Meanwhile, place tamari, miso and vinegar in a bowl and stir until smooth.

Divide rice mixture among bowls and top with soft-boiled egg. Add asparagus, radish, sauerkraut and micro herbs, if using. Drizzle with miso dressing and serve.

Indian breakfast bowl with dill yoghurt and paneer

Serves *4*

1 small cauliflower,
   roughly chopped
2 tbs coconut oil
1 onion, finely chopped
4cm piece (20g) ginger,
   finely chopped
1 tsp each ground turmeric
   and cumin
½ tsp each ground cinnamon
   and dried chilli flakes
10 fresh curry leaves, plus fried
   curry leaves (optional) to serve
100ml coconut cream
250g paneer, cut into thick slices
100ml white vinegar
4 eggs
Chutney, thinly sliced cucumber
   and micro coriander (optional),
   to serve

Dill yoghurt
1½ cups (420g) thick Greek-style
   yoghurt
Juice of ½ a lemon
1 garlic clove, crushed
2 tbs chopped dill

Whip up the spiced cauliflower and the dill yoghurt the night before, then simply cook the eggs and paneer the next morning to serve.

For the dill yoghurt, combine all ingredients in a bowl and season. Chill until needed.

Place the cauliflower in a food processor and whiz until it resembles rice. Melt 1 tbs oil in a large frypan over medium heat. Add the onion and ginger, and cook, stirring, for 5 minutes or until softened. Add spices and curry leaves, and cook for 2 minutes or until fragrant. Add cauliflower and cook, stirring, for 5 minutes or until heated through and coated in spices. Add coconut cream and stir to combine. Cook for a further 2 minutes or until coconut cream has reduced slightly. Keep warm, or chill and reheat.

To cook paneer, heat remaining 1 tbs oil in a non-stick frypan over medium heat. Add paneer and cook for 4 minutes, turning occasionally, or until golden. Drain on paper towel and set aside.

To poach eggs, add vinegar to a large, deep saucepan of boiling water. Turn down to a simmer. Crack 1 egg into a cup and gently pour into water. Cook for 2-3 minutes or until cooked to your liking. Remove with a slotted spoon and drain on paper towel. Repeat with remaining eggs.

Divide cauliflower rice among serving bowls. Drizzle with dill yoghurt and top with paneer, poached eggs, chutney and cucumber. Scatter with fried curry leaves and micro coriander, if using, to serve.

Garlic & olive oil butter beans with smoked salmon

This fast twist on baked beans is rich in protein, B-group vitamins, iron and fibre.

Serves *4*

¼ cup (60ml) olive oil
2 small red chillies, thinly sliced
4 garlic cloves, thinly sliced
½ cup (125ml) chicken stock
400g can butter beans,
   rinsed, drained
½ cup (40g) finely grated
   parmesan, plus extra to serve
100ml white vinegar
4 eggs
4 thick slices bread, toasted, halved
100g smoked salmon, torn
Rocket leaves, to serve

Heat the oil in a saucepan over medium heat. Add chilli and garlic, and cook, stirring, for 2 minutes or until fragrant. Add stock and beans. Cook, stirring, for 4-5 minutes or until warmed through and stock has reduced slightly. Stir in the parmesan and season. Keep warm, or chill and reheat.

To poach eggs, add vinegar to a large, deep saucepan of boiling water. Turn down to a simmer. Crack 1 egg into a cup and gently pour into water. Cook for 2-3 minutes or until cooked to your liking. Remove with a slotted spoon and drain on paper towel. Repeat with remaining eggs.

Divide toast among serving plates. Top with bean mixture, smoked salmon and poached eggs. Scatter with rocket and extra parmesan to serve.

Pecan pie overnight oats (P 28)

Overnight oat & chia pancakes with honey-roasted grapes (P 28)

Overnight soaking is a great technique to soften grains and seeds such as oats and chia – all the work is done while you sleep!

Pecan pie overnight oats

Serves *4-6*
Begin this recipe 1 day ahead.

2½ cups (225g) rolled oats
1L (4 cups) milk, plus extra to serve
1 tsp vanilla extract
½ cup (70g) pecans
1 cup (250ml) maple syrup
Finely grated zest of 2 oranges
Ground cinnamon, to serve

Place oats, milk and vanilla in a large bowl. Cover and chill overnight.

Preheat the oven to 200°C. Line a baking dish with baking paper. Place pecans, half the maple syrup, half the orange zest and 1 tsp salt flakes in prepared dish and toss to combine. Roast for 15 minutes or until pecans are caramelised. Cool to room temperature, then roughly crush. Store in an airtight container until ready to use.

The next day, divide oat mixture among serving bowls and top with pecan mixture. Drizzle with remaining ½ cup (125ml) maple syrup and sprinkle with cinnamon and remaining orange zest. Serve with extra milk.

Overnight oat & chia pancakes with honey-roasted grapes

Makes *10 pancakes*
Begin this recipe 1 day ahead.

1 tbs black chia seeds
½ cup (45g) rolled oats
1 cup (150g) self-raising flour, sifted
4 eggs, separated
½ cup (125ml) runny honey
600ml buttermilk
50g unsalted butter,
  cut into 10 pieces
150g small black grapes
  (we used champagne grapes)
Sour cream, to serve

Place the chia, oats, flour, egg yolks, ¼ cup (60ml) honey, buttermilk and a pinch of salt in a bowl and whisk to combine. Place eggwhites in a separate bowl and whisk to soft peaks. Fold through the buttermilk mixture, cover and chill overnight.

When ready to cook, melt 1 piece of butter in a 22cm non-stick frypan over medium-low heat. Add ½ cup batter and tilt to coat the base. Cook for 8-10 minutes, flipping halfway, or until golden and cooked through. Remove from pan and keep warm. Repeat with remaining butter and batter to make 10 pancakes.

Meanwhile, preheat the oven to 180°C. Line a small baking tray with baking paper. Place grapes and remaining 65ml honey on prepared tray and toss to combine. Roast for 15 minutes or until soft.

Divide warm pancakes among serving plates and spread with sour cream. Top with honey-roasted grapes, fold over and serve.

Genius extras
Morning tea slices

MORNING TEA SLICES

These better-for-you treats contain zero refined sugar and are all gluten free. Store them in the fridge in an airtight container for up to five days.

Spiced carrot cake bars

Makes *about 15 pieces*
Begin this recipe at least 4 hours ahead.

2 carrots, coarsely grated
1 tbs finely grated ginger
½ cup (125ml) melted coconut oil
½ cup (125ml) maple syrup
¼ cup (70g) nut butter
½ cup (45g) desiccated coconut
2 eggs, lightly beaten
1 tsp vanilla extract
1½ cups (150g) hazelnut meal

Cheesecake topping
750g cream cheese, softened
½ cup (125ml) maple syrup
3½ titanium-strength gelatine leaves
½ cup (125ml) coconut cream
1 tsp vanilla extract
1½ cups (150g) hazelnut meal

Preheat the oven to 180°C. Grease a 20cm x 30cm lamington pan and line with baking paper, leaving 5cm overhanging. Combine base ingredients in a bowl and press into prepared pan. Bake for 35 minutes or until golden. Cool completely.

For the topping, place cream cheese in a stand mixer fitted with the paddle attachment and beat until smooth. Add maple syrup and beat to combine. Soak gelatine in cold water for 5 minutes to soften. Place coconut cream and vanilla in a pan over low heat and bring to a simmer. Squeeze excess water from gelatine and stir into coconut cream. Cool, then beat into cream cheese mixture.

Spread topping over base, top with hazelnut meal and chill for 4 hours or until firm. Cut into pieces to serve.

Quinoa & date caramel slice

Makes *about 15 pieces*
Begin this recipe at least 4 hours ahead.

1½ cups (225g) quinoa flour
1 cup (150g) gluten-free plain flour
1 cup (90g) desiccated coconut
½ tsp gluten-free baking powder
½ tsp xanthan gum
   (from health food shops)
350ml maple syrup
100g unsalted butter,
   melted, cooled
1 egg, lightly beaten
450g medjool dates, pitted
1 tsp vanilla bean paste
1 cup (100g) cacao powder
½ cup (125ml) melted coconut oil

Preheat the oven to 180°C. Grease a 20cm x 30cm lamington pan and line with baking paper, leaving 5cm overhanging. To make the base, place flours, coconut, baking powder, xanthan gum, ½ cup (125ml) maple syrup, butter and egg in a bowl and stir to combine. Press into prepared pan and bake for 20 minutes or until golden. Cool completely.

Place dates in a food processor and whiz until very smooth. Add vanilla and 100ml maple syrup, and whiz until a light caramel. Spread over cooled base.

Place cacao powder, coconut oil and remaining ½ cup (125ml) maple syrup in a saucepan over low heat and stir until smooth. Pour over caramel in an even layer and chill for 4 hours or until firm. Cut into pieces to serve.

Chocolate & cherry slice

Makes *about 15 pieces*
Begin this recipe at least 4 hours ahead.

3 cups (300g) almond meal
4½ cups (400g) desiccated coconut
1 cup (250ml) rice malt syrup
1 egg, lightly beaten
1 cup (250ml) melted coconut oil
⅔ cup (100g) dried cherries,
   finely chopped
1 cup (250ml) sugar-free cherry
   juice (from health food shops)
2 tsp vanilla bean paste
200g dark no-sugar-added
   chocolate, melted, cooled slightly

Preheat the oven to 180°C. Grease
a 20cm x 30cm lamington pan and
line with baking paper, leaving
5cm overhanging. To make the
base, combine almond meal,
100g coconut, 100ml rice malt
syrup, egg and ⅓ cup (80ml) oil
in a bowl. Press into prepared pan
and bake for 20 minutes or until
golden. Cool completely.

   Place dried cherry, cherry juice
and vanilla in a food processor with
remaining 300g coconut, 150ml rice
malt syrup and 170ml oil, and whiz
to combine. Press over base. Pour
melted chocolate evenly over cherry
layer and chill for 4 hours or until
firm. Cut into pieces to serve.

Coconut & pistachio rice bars

Makes *about 15 pieces*
Begin this recipe at least 6 hours ahead.

7 cups (140g) puffed brown rice
½ titanium-strength gelatine leaf
½ cup (125ml) coconut cream
1 cup (250ml) melted coconut oil
1 cup (250ml) runny honey
2 tsp vanilla bean paste
Finely grated zest of 1 orange
¾ cup (110g) pistachios,
   finely chopped

Grease a 20cm x 30cm lamington
pan and line with baking paper,
leaving 5cm overhanging. Place
puffed rice in a large bowl. Soak
gelatine in cold water for 5 minutes
to soften. Place coconut cream in
a small saucepan over low heat and
bring to a simmer. Squeeze excess
water from gelatine and stir into
coconut cream. Add oil, honey
and vanilla, and stir to combine.
Cool slightly.

   Add coconut mixture and orange
zest to puffed rice and use your
hands to completely coat. Press
into prepared pan and top with
pistachios. Chill for 6 hours or until
firm. Cut into pieces to serve.

L-R: Pina colada protein balls (P 36)
Prune & hazelnut brownie balls (P 36)
Turkish delight protein balls (P 37)
Vanilla latte protein balls (P 37)

Genius extras
Power snacks

POWER SNACKS

Give yourself a boost with these little powerhouses. Store them in the fridge in an airtight container for up to five days, or freeze them for up to three months.

Pina colada protein balls

Makes *about 22*

2/3 cup (70g) vanilla protein powder
2 cups (200g) almond meal
1½ tsp vanilla bean paste
¼ cup (60ml) rice malt syrup
⅓ cup (80ml) coconut cream
2 tbs coconut oil
2 cups (140g) shredded coconut
1 cup (200g) finely chopped
   fresh pineapple
Finely grated lime zest, to serve

Place protein powder, almond meal, vanilla, rice malt syrup, coconut cream, oil, 1 cup (70g) shredded coconut and pineapple in a food processor and whiz until smooth. Using your hands, roll heaped tablespoons of mixture into balls.

Place remaining 1 cup (70g) shredded coconut in a bowl. Roll balls in coconut, scatter with lime zest and chill for 1 hour to firm up before serving.

Prune & hazelnut brownie balls

Makes *about 20*

25 pitted prunes
½ cup (50g) cacao powder,
   plus extra to dust
1½ cups (150g) hazelnut meal
¼ cup (25g) protein powder
⅓ cup (65g) coconut oil
⅓ cup (80ml) milk
2 tsp vanilla bean paste
½ cup (60g) cacao nibs
2 tbs finely chopped hazelnuts

Place prunes, cacao powder, hazelnut meal, protein powder, oil, milk and vanilla in a food processor and whiz until smooth. Add cacao nibs and whiz until just combined. Using your hands, roll heaped tablespoons of mixture into balls.

Combine hazelnuts and extra cacao powder in a bowl. Roll balls in mixture and chill until ready to serve.

Turkish delight protein balls

Makes *about 16*

½ cup (50g) vanilla protein powder
1 cup (100g) almond meal
1 cup (70g) shredded coconut
1½ tsp vanilla bean paste
2 tbs maple syrup
2 tsp rosewater
¼ cup (50g) coconut oil
1 cup (240g) fresh ricotta
½ cup (75g) crushed pistachios
⅓ cup (50g) freeze-dried
  strawberries, crumbled

Place protein powder, almond meal, shredded coconut, vanilla, maple syrup, rosewater, coconut oil and ricotta in a food processor and whiz until smooth. Using your hands, roll heaped tablespoons of mixture into balls.

Combine pistachios and strawberry in a bowl. Roll balls in mixture and chill until ready to serve.

Vanilla latte protein balls

Makes *about 20*

⅓ cup (35g) vanilla protein powder
2½ cups (250g) almond meal
1½ tsp vanilla bean paste
¼ cup (60ml) rice malt syrup
2 tbs coconut oil
2 tbs milk
¼ cup (60ml) espresso
2 tbs nut butter
⅓ cup (15g) instant coffee powder
½ cup (50g) milk powder

Place protein powder, almond meal, vanilla, rice malt syrup, oil, milk, espresso, nut butter and 2 tbs instant coffee in a bowl and stir to combine. Using your hands, roll heaped tablespoons of mixture into balls.

Combine milk powder and remaining 2 tbs instant coffee in a bowl. Roll balls in mixture and chill until ready to serve.

Chapter Two

Meat-free Mondays

Whether you're a dedicated vegetarian, love the occasional veg-only day or simply want to find enticing recipes for meals without meat, this is the chapter for you. With inventive new ideas for vegie lovers needing inspiration and for those not yet convinced, you may find yourself committing to more than just Mondays...

Carrot felafel with fast tabbouleh, hummus and pickles

A new boost from carrot takes the chickpea felafel up a notch. Added bonus? Leftovers make the perfect lunch tomorrow.

Serves *4*

400g can chickpeas,
  rinsed, drained
2 large (about 360g) carrots,
  coarsely grated
2 tsp garam masala
½ tsp ground turmeric
2 garlic cloves, crushed
2 tbs chopped coriander leaves
1 egg, lightly beaten
½ cup (75g) white sesame seeds
Sunflower oil, to deep-fry
Garlic dip, hummus, pickles and
  Lebanese flatbreads, to serve

Fast tabbouleh
1 bunch each flat-leaf parsley
  and mint, leaves picked,
  finely chopped
250g cherry tomatoes, halved
1 eschalot, finely chopped
1 tsp sumac, plus extra to serve
Juice of 1 lemon
¼ cup (60ml) extra virgin olive oil,
  plus extra to drizzle

For the tabbouleh, combine all ingredients in a bowl. Season and set aside.

To make the felafel, place chickpeas in a food processor and whiz until finely chopped. Transfer to a bowl and add carrot, spices, garlic, coriander and egg. Season.

Using your hands, roll heaped tablespoons of mixture into balls. Place sesame seeds on a plate and roll balls in seeds to coat completely. Chill for 10 minutes to firm up.

Half-fill a deep-fryer or large saucepan with oil and heat to 160°C (a cube of bread will turn golden in 3 minutes when oil is hot enough). In batches, deep-fry the felafel for 6-7 minutes or until golden and crisp. Remove with a slotted spoon and drain on paper towel.

Arrange the dip and tabbouleh on a serving platter and drizzle with extra olive oil. Add felafel, sprinkle with extra sumac and serve with hummus, pickles and flatbreads.

Saffron, butter & tomato spaghetti with burrata

An easy five-ingredient pasta sauce is enriched by the addition of fragrant saffron and burrata, a fresh cow's milk cheese stuffed with stracciatella and cream.

Serves *4*

80g unsalted butter, chopped
600g tomatoes, chopped
3 garlic cloves, chopped
1 cup (250ml) vegetable stock
1 tsp saffron threads
300g spaghetti
2 balls burrata or buffalo
   mozzarella, torn, to serve

Melt butter in a large, deep frypan over medium heat. Add tomato and garlic, and cook, stirring occasionally, for 10 minutes or until tomato begins to break down. Add stock and saffron. Season and cook, breaking up tomato with a wooden spoon, for a further 15 minutes or until thick and reduced. Season to taste.

Meanwhile, cook spaghetti according to packet instructions. Drain and stir through sauce. Divide among serving bowls and serve with burrata and freshly ground black pepper.

Leek, spinach & Taleggio risotto

As well as the classic parmesan, ripe washed-rind cheese infuses this winter risotto with creamy goodness.

Serves *4*

150g baby spinach
1.5L (6 cups) vegetable stock
2 tbs extra virgin olive oil,
  plus extra to drizzle
50g cold unsalted butter, chopped
2 leeks (white part only),
  finely chopped
300g carnaroli or arborio rice
½ cup (125ml) dry white wine
50g finely grated parmesan,
  plus extra to serve
80g Taleggio, rind removed,
  chopped
Baby sorrel leaves (optional),
  to serve

Place spinach and 1 cup (250ml) stock in a blender and whiz to combine. Set aside.

Place remaining 1.25L (5 cups) stock in a saucepan and bring to the boil. Reduce heat to low and keep at a gentle simmer.

Heat the oil and half the butter in a heavy-based saucepan over medium-low heat. Add leek and cook, stirring, for 2-3 minutes or until softened. Add rice and stir for 2 minutes or until well coated in mixture. Add wine and cook, stirring, for a further 30 seconds or until evaporated.

Add hot stock, one ladle at a time, to the pan, stirring continuously and allowing the stock to be absorbed before adding the next, until all stock has been used. Add spinach mixture and stir to combine. Continue to cook, stirring, until the rice is cooked and the mixture is thick; this whole process will take about 20 minutes. The cooked rice should be creamy but still retaining some bite.

Remove from heat and stir through cheeses and remaining 25g butter. Season. Divide among serving bowls, drizzle with extra oil and sprinkle with extra parmesan. Serve immediately with sorrel, if using.

Ricotta & spinach fritters with pea & avocado salad (P 51)

Roasted tomato, chickpea & fennel salad (P 48)
Zucchini caesar salad (P 49)

Roasted tomato, chickpea & fennel salad

Up your salad game by cooking the tomatoes and chickpeas in savoury and aromatic spices, then add the roasting oil to make a genius dressing.

Serves *4*

3 large tomatoes, thickly sliced
250g cherry tomatoes on the vine
400g can chickpeas,
　rinsed, drained
2 garlic cloves, crushed
1½ tsp each fennel seeds,
　cumin seeds and smoked
　paprika (pimenton)
100ml extra virgin olive oil
2 tbs red wine vinegar
1 cup (200g) quinoa, cooked
　according to packet instructions
1 fennel bulb, very thinly sliced
1½ cups (360g) fresh ricotta

Preheat the oven to 200°C. Line a baking tray with baking paper. Arrange all the tomatoes in a single layer on prepared tray, then scatter with chickpeas. Place garlic, spices and oil in a bowl. Season and stir to combine. Drizzle over tomato mixture and roast for 10 minutes or until warmed through.

Drain oil from baking tray into a bowl. Add vinegar and stir to combine. Divide quinoa among serving plates. Add fennel and top with tomato mixture and ricotta. Drizzle with dressing to serve.

Zucchini caesar salad

This vegetarian version of a classic caesar gets its salty flavour from capers rather than anchovies. Try making the dressing using our veganaise (see recipe, p 117).

Serves *4*

½ cup (150g) whole-egg
  mayonnaise
2 tbs capers in vinegar,
  drained, chopped
1 tbs finely grated parmesan,
  plus extra to serve
Juice of 1 lemon
1 small garlic clove, crushed
4 soft-boiled eggs, peeled, halved
2 zucchini, thinly sliced into rounds
1 small butter lettuce, leaves torn
4 slices baguette, toasted

Combine mayonnaise, caper, parmesan, lemon juice and garlic in a bowl and season. Divide egg, zucchini, lettuce and baguette among serving bowls. Drizzle with dressing and scatter with extra parmesan to serve.

Ricotta & spinach fritters with pea & avocado salad

Spanakopita, a Greek vegetarian pie, is the inspiration behind these super-quick fritters.

Serves *4*

500g fresh ricotta
⅓ cup (25g) finely grated
 parmesan
100g feta, crumbled
½ tsp dried mint
¼ cup mint leaves, chopped,
 plus extra leaves to serve
100g baby spinach leaves,
 chopped
1 garlic clove, crushed
1 egg, lightly beaten
⅓ cup (50g) wholemeal flour,
 plus extra to dust
⅓ cup (80ml) extra virgin olive oil

Pea & avocado salad
200g sugar snap peas, blanched,
 refreshed, halved lengthways
½ cup (60g) frozen peas,
 blanched, refreshed
2 cups watercress sprigs
1 avocado, cut into wedges
2 tbs extra virgin olive oil
2 tsp wholegrain mustard
1 tbs organic apple cider vinegar

Place ricotta, parmesan, feta, dried and fresh mint, spinach, garlic, egg and flour in a bowl. Season and stir to combine.

Heat oil in a large frypan over medium heat. Using floured hands, roll 2 tbs ricotta mixture per fritter into balls, then flatten slightly. In batches, add to pan and cook, turning once, for 5 minutes or until golden and crisp. Keep warm.

For the salad, place peas, watercress and avocado in a bowl and toss to combine. To make the dressing, whisk oil, mustard and vinegar in a small bowl. Season.

Arrange fritters on serving plates and top with salad. Drizzle with dressing and sprinkle with extra mint leaves to serve.

Crispy tofu with miso and greens

This Japanese favourite uses pantry-friendly ingredients – a quick stop for groceries and you can have it whenever you fancy.

Serves *2*

1 tbs white (shiro) miso
1 tbs soy sauce
1 tbs mirin
1 tbs rice vinegar
5cm piece (25g) ginger, sliced
1L (4 cups) vegetable stock
300g fresh shiitake mushrooms
300g packet firm silken tofu
¼ cup (35g) cornflour
Sunflower oil, for shallow-frying
½ bunch Chinese spinach
   or English spinach,
   blanched, refreshed
1 cup (100g) frozen podded
   edamame (soybeans),
   blanched, refreshed
Toasted white sesame seeds, thinly
   sliced spring onion and micro red
   shiso (optional), to serve

Combine miso, soy, mirin, vinegar, ginger and stock in a saucepan and place over medium heat. Cook, stirring, until miso dissolves. Add mushrooms and bring to a simmer. Cook for 5 minutes, stirring occasionally, to infuse the stock. Keep warm.

Pat dry tofu with paper towel, removing as much excess liquid as possible. Cut tofu in half horizontally. Coat all sides in cornflour. Heat 2cm oil in a non-stick frypan over medium heat. Carefully add tofu and cook, turning once, for 8 minutes or until crisp and golden.

Arrange spinach in shallow serving bowls and ladle over hot stock mixture. Top with tofu and scatter with edamame, sesame seeds, spring onion and shiso, if using, to serve.

Tandoori pumpkin with cucumber raita (P 56)

Baked gnocchi sugo finto (fake sauce) (P 57)

Tandoori pumpkin with cucumber raita

Classically paired with chicken, tandoori spices also work really well with vegetables. Try this mix with eggplant or cauliflower, too.

Serves *4*

700g Jap pumpkin, cut into wedges
1 tbs tandoori paste
1 tsp garam masala
2 tbs olive oil, plus extra to drizzle
Warm naan and coriander sprigs,
    to serve

Cucumber raita
1 cup (280g) thick Greek-style
    yoghurt
1 Lebanese cucumber,
    coarsely grated
1 garlic clove, crushed
Juice of 1 lime

Preheat the oven to 200°C. Line a baking tray with baking paper. Arrange pumpkin in a single layer on prepared tray. Combine the tandoori paste, garam masala and oil in a bowl. Drizzle over pumpkin and season. Roast for 40 minutes or until tender.

For the cucumber raita, combine yoghurt, cucumber, garlic and lime juice in a bowl. Season and drizzle with extra oil.

Arrange pumpkin on a serving platter. To serve, spread pumpkin on naan, sprinkle with coriander sprigs and serve with raita.

Baked gnocchi sugo finto (fake sauce)

Sugo finto is a Tuscan peasant sauce in which vegetables are finely chopped to emulate meat, while loads of herbs add a rich flavour of ragu.

Serves *4*

⅓ cup (80ml) extra virgin olive oil
2 celery stalks, finely chopped
1 large carrot, finely chopped
1 onion, finely chopped
3 garlic cloves, finely chopped
1 tbs fennel seeds
1 tsp dried chilli flakes
2 tbs tomato paste
½ bunch oregano, leaves picked,
    finely chopped
½ bunch rosemary, leaves picked,
    finely chopped, plus extra
    leaves to serve
1 bunch sage, leaves picked,
    finely chopped, plus fried
    sage leaves to serve
700ml tomato sugo
500g store-bought gnocchi,
    cooked according to
    packet instructions
1 cup (250g) mascarpone
100g coarsely grated cheddar

Heat oil in a large saucepan over medium heat. Add celery, carrot and onion, and cook, stirring occasionally, for 12 minutes or until softened. Add garlic, fennel seeds, chilli, tomato paste and herbs, and cook, stirring, for 2 minutes or until fragrant. Add sugo and 1 cup (250ml) water and reduce heat to low. Simmer, stirring occasionally, for 25 minutes or until thick and reduced. Season.

Preheat the oven to 200°C. Stir gnocchi through sauce and divide among 4 individual baking dishes or place in 1 large dish. Combine mascarpone and cheddar in a bowl and season. Dollop over gnocchi mixture and bake for 20 minutes or until golden and bubbling.

Scatter with extra rosemary and fried sage leaves to serve.

Smoky eggplant chilli beans

With all the flavours of family-favourite chilli con carne, there's nothing lost here without the mince. This is the one to sneak in front of even the most dedicated carnivore!

Serves *4*

⅓ cup (80ml) extra virgin olive oil
2 eggplants, chopped
1 red capsicum, chopped
400g can chopped tomatoes
2 tbs caramelised onion
   (from delis and supermarkets)
1½ tsp each ground cumin,
   coriander and smoked
   paprika (pimenton)
1 tsp dried chilli flakes
400g can red kidney beans,
   rinsed, drained
1 cup (250ml) vegetable stock
Finely grated cheddar, avocado
   wedges, sliced green chilli,
   coriander sprigs, toasted corn
   tortillas and sour cream, to serve

Heat oil in a large saucepan over medium-high heat. Add eggplant and cook, turning frequently, for 15 minutes or until golden. Using a slotted spoon, transfer to a tray and set aside.

Add capsicum to the pan and cook, turning frequently, for 3-4 minutes or until tender. Add tomato, onion, spices, kidney beans, stock and ½ cup (125ml) water. Simmer for 25 minutes or until thick and reduced.

Return eggplant to pan and cook for 10 minutes or until tender and cooked through. Season. Divide among serving bowls and top with cheese, avocado, green chilli and coriander. Serve with tortillas and sour cream.

Rosemary, root vegetable & creme fraiche dhal

Skip the Indian spices and swap in healthy root vegies and fragrant herbs for seasoning in this twist on warming dhal.

Serves *4*

2 tbs olive oil, plus extra to drizzle
1 onion, finely chopped
3 garlic cloves, finely chopped
1 cup (200g) red lentils, rinsed
3 cups (750ml) vegetable stock
1 large carrot, coarsely grated
1 small parsnip, coarsely grated
1 small sweet potato,
　coarsely grated
1 tbs each finely chopped rosemary
　and sage leaves, plus extra
　chopped leaves to serve
⅓ cup (80g) creme fraiche,
　plus extra to serve
Toasted chopped hazelnuts,
　to serve

Heat the oil in a saucepan over medium heat. Add onion and cook, stirring, for 3-4 minutes or until softened. Add garlic and cook, stirring, for 1 minute or until fragrant. Add lentils, stock, carrot, parsnip and sweet potato. Cook, stirring, for 15 minutes or until lentils are tender. Add the herbs and creme fraiche, and stir to combine. Season.

Divide dhal among serving bowls. Swirl through extra creme fraiche and drizzle with extra oil. Season. Scatter with hazelnuts and sprinkle with extra rosemary and sage to serve.

L-R: Bread & butter pickles (P 64)
Pink peppercorn radishes (P 64)
Indian-style carrot pickle (P 65)
Pickled spring onions (P 65)

Genius extras
Quickles

QUICKLES
(QUICK PICKLES)

For immediate consumption, simply store these in the fridge in a non-reactive container or bowl. If you intend to keep them for longer, you can preserve them, unopened, in a sterilised jar for up to six months (for instructions, see p 188).

Bread & butter pickles

Makes *500ml jar*

1 telegraph cucumber, thinly sliced
3 eschalots, thinly sliced
1 cup (250ml) organic apple
   cider vinegar
½ cup (110g) caster sugar
2 tsp dried chilli flakes, crumbled
2 tsp each fennel and coriander
   seeds, toasted
¼ cup dill sprigs

Place cucumber and eschalot in a non-reactive bowl with 2 tbs salt flakes and toss to combine. Set aside for 30 minutes to soften. Rinse under cold water and drain.
   Place vinegar, sugar and spices in a saucepan over medium heat and stir until sugar dissolves. Bring to the boil. Layer the vegetables and dill in a clean heatproof jar or container and pour over hot pickling mixture. Seal lid and set aside for at least 2 days in a cool, dark place to pickle. Once opened, pickles will keep chilled for up to 3 months.

Pink peppercorn radishes

Makes *800ml jar*

3 bunches radishes, trimmed,
   halved or quartered
1 cup radish leaves
   (from radish bunches)
2 cups (500ml) rice vinegar
2 tbs pink peppercorns
⅓ cup (75g) caster sugar

Wash radish and leaves, and thoroughly dry. Arrange in a clean heatproof jar or container. Place the vinegar, peppercorns, sugar and 1 tbs salt flakes in a saucepan over medium heat and stir until sugar dissolves. Bring to the boil, then cool to lukewarm. Pour over radish mixture, seal lid and set aside in the fridge for 1-10 days before serving. Once opened, pickles will keep chilled for up to 2 months.

Indian-style carrot pickle

Makes *800ml jar*

3 cups (750ml) rice vinegar
½ cup (110g) caster sugar
1 tsp brown mustard seeds
1 tsp coriander seeds, toasted
½ tsp ground turmeric
4 cardamom pods, toasted
2 dried chillies, crumbled
⅓ cup fresh curry leaves
1kg carrots, thinly sliced
    into long matchsticks
    (we used a julienne peeler)

Place vinegar, sugar, mustard seeds, coriander seeds, turmeric, cardamom pods and chilli in a saucepan over medium heat and stir until sugar dissolves. Bring to the boil. Arrange curry leaves and carrot in a clean heatproof jar or container and pour over hot pickling mixture. Cool to room temperature, then seal lid and set aside in the fridge for 1-10 days before serving. Once opened, pickles will keep chilled for up to 3 months.

Pickled spring onions

Makes *800ml jar*

2½ cups (625ml) organic
    apple cider vinegar
3 tsp caraway seeds
1 tsp black peppercorns
⅓ cup (75g) caster sugar
3 bunches spring onions

Place vinegar, caraway seeds, peppercorns, sugar and 1 tbs salt flakes in a saucepan over medium heat and stir until sugar dissolves. Bring to the boil.

Trim tops and ends of spring onions to fit the length of a clean heatproof jar. Arrange in the jar and pour over hot pickling mixture. Seal lid and set aside for at least 3 days in a cool, dark place to pickle. Once opened, pickles will keep chilled for up to 3 months.

Chapter Three

Easy pastry & dough

In this chapter you'll find recipes for homemade pastry as well as those using store-bought, so you can take your pick depending on the time you have. Plus, you can't go past the no-knead overnight dough that will change your life – and put pizza on the menu as often as you like!

Quick tomato & nduja tart with felafel spices

Serves *4-6*

445g frozen Carême Sour Cream
  Shortcrust Pastry, thawed, or
  1 quantity flaky savoury pastry
  (see recipe, p 86)
1 tbs finely grated parmesan
2 tsp zaatar (Middle Eastern
  spice blend – from delis
  and selected supermarkets)
100g nduja (spicy, spreadable
  Italian salami – from delis
  and gourmet food shops)
600g mixed tomatoes,
  larger ones sliced
½ tsp each sumac, ground
  coriander and garam masala
Watercress sprigs and lemon
  wedges, to serve

Dressing
Juice of ½ a lemon
2 tbs extra virgin olive oil
1 garlic clove, crushed

Been wondering what that spreadable salami starting to appear on charcuterie boards is? It's nduja – used as the ultimate easy topping for this super-fast, delicious tart. Watch out, it is pretty spicy.

Preheat oven to 200°C. Line a large baking tray with baking paper. Place pastry on prepared tray and scatter with parmesan and 1 tsp zaatar. Smear nduja over pastry. Place tomatoes in a bowl and toss with sumac, coriander and garam masala. Season. Arrange tomato mixture over pastry, leaving a 2cm border. Fold over pastry edges and bake for 25 minutes or until golden.

Meanwhile, for the dressing, whisk all ingredients together in a small bowl.

Drizzle dressing over hot tart and scatter with watercress and remaining 1 tsp zaatar. Cut into pieces and serve with lemon wedges.

Banana pecan tart with bourbon and burnt butterscotch

Puff pastry is laborious to make so it's a great one to buy and keep in the freezer for no-fuss baking. It makes this impressive-looking tart quick and easy to whip up for guests.

Serves *8*

375g frozen Carême All Butter
    Puff Pastry, thawed
100g pecans, finely chopped
¼ cup (60g) firmly packed
    brown sugar
100g sour cream
⅔ cup (100g) plain flour
2 tsp vanilla bean paste
1 egg, lightly beaten
4 bananas, halved lengthways
Vanilla ice cream, to serve

Bourbon and burnt butterscotch
100g unsalted butter, chopped
⅔ cup (165ml) pure (thin) cream
150g brown sugar
100ml bourbon

Preheat the oven to 200°C. Line a 24cm, 5cm-deep tart pan with the pastry, trimming excess, then chill for 10 minutes. Line with baking paper and fill with pastry weights. Place on a baking tray and bake for 20 minutes or until light golden. Remove paper and weights, and prick the base with a fork. Bake for a further 10 minutes or until pastry is golden and dry. If the pastry has puffed up, use the back of a spoon to press it back into the pan. Set aside to cool slightly.

Combine pecans, 50g brown sugar, sour cream, flour, vanilla and egg in a bowl, then spread over pastry base. Arrange banana over filling and sprinkle with remaining 10g sugar. Bake for 35-40 minutes or until caramelised.

Meanwhile, for the sauce, place butter in a saucepan over medium heat and cook for 6 minutes or until nut-brown. Remove from heat and add remaining ingredients with a pinch of salt flakes. Return to heat and cook, stirring to dissolve sugar, for 5 minutes or until slightly reduced. Drizzle over tart and serve with ice cream.

Rosemary & spelt quiche Lorraine (P 74)

'French onion' & raclette tart (P 75)

Rosemary & spelt quiche Lorraine

Rosemary and spelt flour add an earthy, herbaceous twist to a classic quiche Lorraine.

Serves *8*

1 onion, finely chopped
100g thin slices prosciutto
1 cup (250ml) pure (thin) cream
8 eggs
1 garlic clove, crushed
2 tbs finely chopped rosemary
  leaves, plus extra whole leaves
  to sprinkle
100g each coarsely grated Gruyere
  and fontina cheese
Mixed salad leaves, to serve

Spelt pastry

2 cups (300g) white spelt flour,
  plus extra to dust
150g cold unsalted butter, chopped
1 tbs finely chopped rosemary
  leaves
1 tbs organic apple cider vinegar

For the pastry, place flour and a pinch of salt flakes in a large bowl. Using your fingers, rub in butter until it resembles coarse crumbs. Add the rosemary. Combine vinegar and ⅓ cup (80ml) water in a jug with 4 ice cubes. Fold into flour mixture until pastry comes together in a shaggy dough. Enclose in plastic wrap and chill for 2 hours.

Place onion in a non-stick frypan. Roughly chop half the prosciutto and add to pan. Place over medium heat and cook, stirring, for 10 minutes or until onion has softened and prosciutto is crisp. Transfer to a bowl and set aside to cool completely.

Preheat the oven to 200°C. Roll out pastry on a lightly floured work surface to 3mm thick and use to line a 24cm, 5cm-deep fluted tart pan, trimming excess. Line with baking paper and fill with pastry weights. Place on a baking tray and bake for 25 minutes or until light golden. Remove paper and weights, and bake for a further 10 minutes or until base is golden and dry.

Place cream in a saucepan over medium heat and bring to just below boiling point. Whisk the eggs in a large heatproof bowl. Pour hot cream over egg, whisking constantly to combine. Add garlic, rosemary and the onion mixture. Stir to combine.

Reduce oven temperature to 150°C. Pour filling into pastry case and scatter with cheeses. Arrange remaining 50g prosciutto over the top and sprinkle with extra rosemary leaves. Bake for 45 minutes or until just set. Cool to room temperature. Scatter with salad leaves and serve.

'French onion' & raclette tart

Store-bought French onion dip is the secret ingredient in this luscious tart, adding great flavour with no hassle.

Serves *8*

445g frozen Carême Sour Cream
    Shortcrust Pastry, thawed, or
    1 quantity flaky savoury pastry
    (see recipe, p 86)
50g unsalted butter
5 eschalots, finely chopped
2 tsp caraway seeds
200g store-bought French onion dip
4 eggs, lightly beaten
3/4 cup (180ml) pure (thin) cream
100g raclette cheese (from delis
    – substitute with Gruyere),
    thinly sliced
1 bunch spring onions, blanched,
    refreshed, well dried
Salsa verde (optional, see recipe,
    p 116), to serve

Use pastry to line a 24cm, 5cm-deep fluted tart pan, trimming excess. Chill until needed.

Preheat oven to 200°C. Line pastry case with baking paper and fill with pastry weights. Place on a baking tray and bake for 20 minutes or until light golden. Remove paper and weights, and bake for a further 10 minutes or until base is golden and dry. Set aside to cool slightly.

Meanwhile, melt the butter in a saucepan over low heat. Add eschalot and caraway seeds, and cook, stirring, for 10 minutes or until soft and golden. Set aside.

Place the dip and egg in a bowl and whisk to combine. Add the cream and whisk well. Season.

Spread eschalot mixture over the pastry base, then pour over egg mixture. Arrange cheese slices, then spring onions, over the top. Bake for 1 hour or until the centre is set. Cool to room temperature, then serve with salsa verde, if using.

Silverbeet, ricotta & pancetta pie

This recipe is inspired by an Italian erbazzone, a traditional savoury pie that had its origins in 'cucina povera', or 'poor cuisine'.

Serves *6*

4 slices flat pancetta (from Italian delis) or streaky bacon, chopped
2 eschalots, thinly sliced
2 garlic cloves, roughly chopped
1 bunch silverbeet, stems removed, leaves shredded
½ bunch flat-leaf parsley, leaves picked
1¼ cups (100g) finely grated parmesan, plus extra to sprinkle
1⅔ cups (400g) fresh ricotta, drained of any excess liquid
2 x 445g frozen Carême Sour Cream Shortcrust Pastry, thawed, or 2 quantities flaky savoury pastry (see recipe, p 86)
1 egg, lightly beaten
Micro basil (optional) and lemon wedges, to serve

Preheat the oven to 200°C. Line a baking tray with baking paper. Place pancetta, eschalot and garlic in a large frypan over medium heat. Cook, stirring, for 5 minutes or until soft. Add silverbeet and parsley, and cook, stirring, for 5 minutes or until wilted. Season. Fold through cheeses, then remove from heat.

Place 1 pastry sheet on prepared tray. Spoon over filling, leaving a 6cm border. Top with remaining pastry sheet. Trim corners to make them rounded, then use your fingers to press pastry edges together to seal.

Combine egg with 1 tbs water, then brush egg mixture over pastry. Sprinkle with extra parmesan and bake for 55 minutes or until pastry is golden and cooked. Set aside to cool slightly.

Sprinkle warm pie with micro basil, if using, and serve with lemon wedges.

Chilli beef & sweet potato pie (P 80)

Fried apple & cinnamon hand pies (P 81)

Chilli beef & sweet potato pie

Low-GI sweet potato and a hit of heat revamp the Aussie classic meat pie. This chilli beef is also great as a nacho topping.

Serves *6-8*

⅓ cup (80ml) extra virgin olive oil
1 onion, finely chopped
1 red capsicum, finely chopped
1 long red chilli, finely chopped
2 garlic cloves, crushed
2 tbs tomato paste
2 tsp each ground cumin, ground
    coriander and fennel seeds
2 tsp smoked paprika (pimenton),
    plus extra to sprinkle
1½ tsp dried chilli flakes
1kg beef mince
410g can tomato puree
2 cups (500ml) beef stock
1 large (about 800g) sweet
    potato, halved
150g sour cream
375g frozen Carême All Butter
    Puff Pastry, thawed
1 egg, lightly beaten
Slaw, sliced green chilli, coriander
    leaves, lime halves and bread
    & butter pickles (optional,
    see recipe, p 64), to serve

Heat the oil in a large saucepan over medium heat. Add onion, capsicum and chilli. Cook, stirring, for 6 minutes or until softened. Add garlic and cook for 1 minute or until fragrant. Add tomato paste and spices, and cook, stirring, for 2 minutes or until fragrant. Add mince and cook, breaking up with a wooden spoon, for 15 minutes or until browned all over. Add tomato puree and stock, and bring to a simmer. Cook, stirring occasionally, for 30 minutes or until thick and reduced. Season.

Meanwhile, preheat the oven to 200°C. Wrap each sweet potato half in microwave-safe plastic wrap and microwave on high for 10 minutes or until very tender (alternatively, steam until tender). Remove from plastic wrap, scoop out flesh, discarding skins, and mash with sour cream. Season sweet potato mixture and spread into the base of a 2L (8-cup) baking dish. Spoon mince mixture over the top.

Roll out pastry on a lightly floured work surface and use to cover mince mixture, trimming excess. Press edges to seal. Combine egg with 1 tbs water, then brush egg mixture over pastry. Sprinkle with salt flakes and extra paprika. Make a few small incisions in the pastry to allow steam to escape. Place on a baking tray and bake for 35 minutes or until golden and bubbling. Set aside for 15 minutes to rest before serving.

Serve pie hot with slaw, chilli, coriander, lime halves and pickles, if using.

Fried apple & cinnamon hand pies

Once prepared, you can keep these pies in the freezer for up to one month, then simply fry until golden and cooked through.

Makes *8*

Begin this recipe at least 4 hours ahead.

4 cups (600g) plain flour,
    plus extra to dust
200g cold unsalted butter, chopped
300ml cold milk
1 tbs organic apple cider vinegar
1 egg, lightly beaten
Sunflower oil, for shallow-frying
Caster sugar and ground
    cinnamon, to dust
Double cream, to serve

Apple jam
50g unsalted butter, chopped
5 (about 1kg) Granny Smith apples,
    peeled, cored, cut into 1cm pieces
2 tsp vanilla bean paste
2/3 cup (150g) caster sugar
100g brown sugar
1 tsp ground cinnamon
1/2 tsp each ground nutmeg
    and cloves
Finely grated zest and
    juice of 1 lemon

To make the pastry, place flour and a pinch of salt flakes in a large bowl. Using your fingers, rub in butter until it resembles coarse crumbs. Add milk and vinegar, and stir to combine, then knead until the mixture just forms a dough. Enclose in plastic wrap and chill for 3 hours.

For the apple jam, melt butter in a heavy-based saucepan over medium heat. Add apple, vanilla, sugars, spices and lemon zest and juice. Cook, stirring occasionally, for 30 minutes or until apple is soft and liquid has reduced.

Roll out pastry on a lightly floured work surface to 3mm thick. Cut eight 12cm x 15cm rectangles from pastry. Place 2 tbs apple jam in the centre of each pastry piece. Brush edges with egg, then fold over and press to seal. Transfer to a tray and freeze for 1 hour.

Heat 3cm oil in a deep frypan over medium heat and bring to 160°C (a cube of bread will turn golden in 3 minutes when the oil is hot enough). Working in batches, fry pies for 10 minutes, turning halfway, or until golden and cooked through. Remove and drain on paper towel, then dust with sugar and cinnamon while still hot. Serve with cream.

Peach tart with caramelised passionfruit honey

Serves *8-10*

1 quantity ultimate sweet tart
   pastry (see recipe, page 86)
500g yellow peaches, stones
   removed, cut into wedges
150ml runny honey
1 egg, lightly beaten
1 tbs demerara sugar
Pulp of 3 passionfruit

Frangipane filling
100g sour cream
1 tsp vanilla extract
50ml runny honey
1 egg, lightly beaten
½ cup (75g) plain flour,
   plus extra to dust
½ cup (50g) almond meal

This simple free-form tart cuts corners by using a fast frangipane filling. It's equally delicious with in-season nectarines or plums.

Grease a large baking tray and line with baking paper. Roll out pastry on a lightly floured work surface to form a 3mm-thick, 20cm x 40cm oval, using a paring knife to round the edges. Transfer pastry to prepared tray and chill until needed.

For the frangipane filling, combine all ingredients in a bowl. Spread over pastry, leaving an 8cm border.

Toss peach with 50ml honey, then arrange over filling. Fold in pastry edges, brush with beaten egg and scatter with sugar. Chill for 15 minutes.

Preheat oven to 200°C. Bake tart for 30 minutes or until golden, then reduce oven to 180°C and bake for a further 30 minutes or until dark golden and cooked through. Remove from oven and set aside to cool slightly.

Meanwhile, to make passionfruit honey, place passionfruit pulp and remaining 100ml honey in a small saucepan over high heat. Bring to a simmer and cook, swirling the pan, until honey is dark and fragrant. Cool to room temperature, then drizzle over the warm tart. Cut into pieces and serve.

Blueberry, orange & gin-spiked galette

Spike this fruit compote with gin for a grown-up twist. Adults only!

Serves *8*

1 quantity ultimate sweet tart
   pastry (see recipe, page 86)
2½ cups (375g) blueberries
1 cup (220g) caster sugar
Finely grated zest of 1 orange,
   plus juice of 2 oranges
½ cup (125ml) gin
2 tbs cornflour
½ cup (75g) hazelnuts, crushed
1 egg, lightly beaten
1 tbs demerara sugar
Double cream, to serve

Grease a baking tray and line with baking paper. Roll out pastry on a lightly floured work surface to form a 3mm-thick, 35cm round. Transfer to prepared tray and set aside.

Place 1 ⅔ cups (250g) blueberries, caster sugar, orange zest and juice, and 2 tbs gin in a saucepan over medium heat. Cook, stirring occasionally, for 10 minutes or until blueberries have broken down. Remove ⅓ cup (80ml) liquid and place in a small bowl. Add cornflour and stir until smooth. Add mixture to saucepan and cook for 2-3 minutes or until thickened slightly. Remove

from heat and set aside to cool. When room temperature, fold through the remaining 125g blueberries and 85ml gin.

Preheat oven to 220°C. Scatter hazelnuts over pastry, leaving a 12cm border. Spoon blueberry mixture over nuts. Fold over pastry edges to create a 6cm border, then fold over border to partially enclose filling. Brush pastry with egg, then sprinkle with demerara sugar.

Bake for 25 minutes, then reduce oven to 180°C and bake for a further 20 minutes or until pastry is golden. Cut into pieces and serve with cream.

Be sure to chill shortcrust pastry for at least two hours before baking – this will stop the butter from splitting during cooking and allows the gluten to relax. Pastry will keep in the fridge, enclosed in plastic wrap, for up to four days, or in the freezer for up to one month. Defrost in the fridge before using.

Ultimate sweet tart pastry

Makes *500g*

2 tsp organic apple cider vinegar
1²/₃ cups (250g) plain flour,
   plus extra to dust
¼ cup (55g) caster sugar
½ vanilla bean, split, seeds scraped
125g cold unsalted butter, chopped
2 tbs sour cream

Combine vinegar and ¼ cup (60ml) iced water in a jug. Place flour in a large bowl with sugar, vanilla seeds and a pinch of salt flakes. Add butter and toss to coat, then rub into flour mixture, leaving some larger pieces (this will make the pastry nice and flaky). Stir in sour cream, then gradually add vinegar mixture, bringing the dough together with your hands (don't add extra water – the dough will be quite shaggy but will come together once chilled).

Turn out onto a lightly floured work surface and gently knead. Enclose in plastic wrap and chill for at least 2 hours before using.

Flaky savoury pastry

Makes *650g*

2¹/₃ cups (350g) plain flour,
   plus extra to dust
200g cold unsalted butter, chopped
¼ cup (60ml) organic apple
   cider vinegar

Place flour and 1 tsp salt flakes in a bowl. Add butter and toss to coat. Using a flat-bladed knife or pastry cutter, roughly cut in butter, leaving some larger pieces (this will make the pastry nice and flaky).

Combine vinegar and ¼ cup (60ml) iced water in a jug. In 3 batches, add to flour mixture, stirring to combine.

Turn out onto a lightly floured work surface and gently knead until dough comes together. Enclose in plastic wrap and chill for at least 2 hours before using.

L-R: Spiced lamb mince pizza (P 90)
Speck, mushroom & fontina pizza (P 91)
Eggplant parmigiana pizza (P 91)

Genius extras
Fast pizzas

FAST PIZZAS

This dough is a cinch to mix together the night before, and the bases can be pre-baked up to four hours before using. To store unbaked dough for later use, individually enclose dough pieces in plastic wrap and chill for up to seven days.

No-knead overnight pizza dough

Makes *4 x 28cm pizza bases*
Begin this recipe 1 day ahead.

4 cups (600g) plain flour,
    plus extra to dust
1 tsp (5g) dried yeast
Fine semolina, to dust

Place flour and yeast in a bowl with a large pinch of salt flakes. Add 1¾ cups (430ml) water and stir to combine. Transfer to a lightly oiled bowl, cover with plastic wrap and set aside overnight at room temperature to rest.

The next day, preheat the oven to 220°C. Dust pizza trays with semolina. Divide dough into 4 even pieces. Roll out 1 piece of dough on a lightly floured work surface to form a 28cm round. Transfer to a prepared tray, prick all over with a fork and bake for 12-15 minutes or until light golden. Repeat with remaining dough. (If you only have 1 or 2 trays, allow cooked base to cool slightly, then transfer to a wire rack. Dust tray with semolina and repeat with another round of dough.)

To make pizza, add toppings and return to oven according to recipe instructions.

Spiced lamb mince pizzas

Makes *2 pizzas*

2 pre-baked pizza bases
2 tbs olive oil
5 garlic cloves, chopped
500g cherry tomatoes, halved
¼ cup (70g) tomato paste
1 tbs sumac
1½ tsp smoked paprika (pimenton)
2 tsp dried chilli flakes
500g lean lamb mince
¼ cup (70g) tahini
Juice of 1 lemon
70g pine nuts, toasted, chopped
Purple radish or flat-leaf parsley
    leaves, to serve

Preheat the oven to 220°C. Line 2 pizza trays with baking paper and place 1 pre-baked base on each tray.

To make the topping, heat oil in a frypan over medium-low heat. Add garlic and cook, stirring, for 2 minutes or until fragrant. Add tomato and cook, crushing with a wooden spoon, for 15 minutes or until liquid is slightly reduced. Add tomato paste, sumac, paprika and chilli. Season. Cook, stirring, for 5 minutes or until lightly caramelised. Set aside to cool.

Place mince in a bowl. Season, add cooled tomato mixture and use your hands to combine.

Divide lamb mixture between pizza bases. Bake for 15 minutes or until lamb is cooked and bases are crisp.

Whisk tahini and lemon juice in a bowl with ⅓ cup (80ml) warm water. Season. Drizzle over pizzas, then scatter with pine nuts and radish leaves. Cut into pieces and serve.

Speck, mushroom & fontina pizzas

Makes *2 pizzas*

2 pre-baked pizza bases
1 small desiree potato,
   scrubbed, very thinly sliced
2 tbs olive oil
600g mixed mushrooms, sliced
1 garlic clove, crushed
100g speck, finely chopped
200g fontina cheese, thinly sliced
½ bunch sage, leaves picked
Juice of ½ a lemon, to serve

Preheat the oven to 250°C. Line
2 pizza trays with baking paper and
place 1 pre-baked base on each tray.
   Toss potato in a bowl with 1 tbs oil.
Season. Arrange evenly over pizza
bases. Place mushroom in the bowl
with garlic and remaining 1 tbs oil.
Season and toss to combine.
Scatter over bases with the speck
and cheese. Bake for 15 minutes,
adding sage in the last 5 minutes,
or until potato is cooked and bases
are crisp. Cut into pieces and
drizzle with lemon juice to serve.

Eggplant parmigiana pizzas

Makes *2 pizzas*

2 pre-baked pizza bases
⅓ cup (80ml) olive oil
2 small eggplants, cut lengthways
   into 5mm-thick slices
1 cup (250ml) tomato passata
3 garlic cloves, crushed
1 tbs fennel seeds, toasted, ground
1 cup (80g) finely grated parmesan
1 bunch oregano, leaves picked
2 tbs extra virgin olive oil
2 x 125g balls buffalo mozzarella
Micro basil or small basil
   leaves, to serve

Preheat the oven to 250°C. Line
2 pizza trays with baking paper and
place 1 pre-baked base on each tray.
   Heat olive oil in a large non-stick
frypan over medium heat. Add
eggplant and cook, turning, for
10 minutes or until golden and
tender. Drain and set aside.
   Spread passata over pizza bases,
then sprinkle with garlic, fennel
seeds, parmesan and oregano.
Arrange eggplant over the top
and drizzle with extra virgin olive
oil. Season. Tear mozzarella and
scatter over pizzas.
   Bake for 15 minutes or until
bases are crisp. Cut into pieces
and scatter with basil to serve.

Chapter Four

Weeknight essentials

We all have our favourite go-to recipes for quick, easy and delicious meals during the week, but keeping the same dishes on high rotation can get a little tired. Find inspiration in the following pages and give your repertoire a revamp without adding any extra hassle in the kitchen.

Satay schnitzels with fried snake beans and pickled cucumber

Give the ultimate midweek meal an Asian twist with satay flavours. The punchy satay mixture is also great with chicken or beef skewers.

Serves *4*

2½ tsp caster sugar
¼ cup (60ml) organic apple
  cider vinegar
1 telegraph cucumber, thinly sliced
⅓ cup (95g) almond butter
¾ cup (180ml) coconut milk
1 garlic clove, crushed
⅓ cup (80ml) soy sauce
Juice of 1 lime
1½ tbs sambal oelek (Indonesian
  chilli paste – from Asian food
  shops and selected supermarkets)
  or chilli bean paste
2 (about 360g) skinless chicken
  breast fillets
⅓ cup (50g) plain flour
1 cup (300g) whole-egg mayonnaise
3 cups (210g) fresh breadcrumbs
Sunflower oil, for shallow-frying
350g snake beans or
  green beans, chopped
Micro red shiso or finely chopped
  coriander leaves, to serve

To make the pickled cucumber, place 1 tsp sugar in a bowl. Add vinegar and 2 tsp salt flakes, and stir until sugar dissolves. Add cucumber and stir to coat. Set aside.

To make the satay mixture, place almond butter, coconut milk, garlic and soy in a saucepan with remaining 1½ tsp sugar. Place over low heat and cook, stirring, for 5 minutes or until warm. Stir through lime juice and 2 tsp sambal oelek, and season. Set aside.

Thinly slice chicken lengthways to about 8mm thick. Place the flour, mayonnaise and breadcrumbs in 3 separate bowls. Coat chicken in flour, then in mayonnaise, then breadcrumbs. Chill until ready to use.

Heat 1cm oil in a large non-stick frypan over medium-high heat. Add chicken, in batches if necessary, and cook for 5 minutes each side or until golden and crisp. Drain on paper towel and keep warm.

Discard oil and wipe out pan. Heat 1 tbs oil in the pan. Add beans and remaining 1 tbs sambal oelek. Cook, tossing, for 2-3 minutes or until beans are just cooked.

Divide schnitzels among serving plates. Add pickled cucumber and bean mixture, and sprinkle with micro shiso or coriander. Serve with satay mixture.

Spiced lamb cutlets with fattoush salad

Smother lamb in store-bought eggplant pickle to add a sweet and tangy flavour with very little effort.

Serves *4*

1 tbs extra virgin olive oil
2 x 4-cutlet French-trimmed
  lamb racks
2 tbs eggplant pickle
  (we used Patak's)
1 tsp each ground cumin, ground
  coriander and fennel seeds

Fattoush salad
1 bunch radishes, trimmed, chopped
4 heirloom tomatoes, sliced
125g cherry tomatoes, halved
½ telegraph cucumber, chopped
½ bunch basil, leaves picked
2 Lebanese flatbreads, toasted
¼ cup (60ml) extra virgin olive oil
Juice of 1 lemon
1 garlic clove, finely chopped

Preheat the oven to 200°C. Line a baking tray with baking paper. Heat 1 tbs oil in a non-stick frypan over medium-high heat. Season lamb and add to pan. Cook, turning occasionally, for 8 minutes or until browned all over. Transfer lamb, fat-side up, to prepared tray. Spread with eggplant pickle and sprinkle with spices. Bake for 15-18 minutes for medium-rare or until lamb is cooked to your liking. Loosely cover with foil and set aside for 5 minutes to rest.

Meanwhile, for the salad, combine radish, tomato, cucumber and basil in a large bowl. Tear flatbreads into large pieces and add to salad. Whisk oil, lemon juice and garlic in a small bowl. Season. Drizzle over salad and serve with lamb.

Roast chicken pasta with sage, oregano & almond pesto

Give your pesto an update by simply adding new herbs and nuts.

Serves *4*

1 bunch each sage, oregano and
   flat-leaf parsley, leaves picked
1/3 cup (55g) almonds, toasted
1 garlic clove, roughly chopped
1/2 tsp dried chilli flakes
1/2 cup (40g) finely grated
   parmesan, plus extra to serve
Finely grated zest and
   juice of 1/2 a lemon
150ml extra virgin olive oil
300g strozzapreti or fusilli pasta
1 barbecued chicken, skin and
   bones removed, meat shredded

Place herbs in a food processor and whiz until finely chopped. Add almonds, garlic, chilli, parmesan, lemon zest and juice, and oil, and whiz to combine. Season.

Cook pasta according to packet instructions. Drain, reserving 1/3 cup (80ml) cooking water.

Return pasta to saucepan and fold through pesto, adding reserved cooking water to loosen. Fold through chicken. Divide among serving bowls, sprinkle with extra parmesan and serve.

Salmon & buckwheat poke bowl with charred spring onions (P 102)

Kale, prosciutto & goat's cheese fritters with green goddess dressing (P 103)

Salmon & buckwheat poke bowl with charred spring onions

A poke (pronounced POH-keh) bowl is a traditional Hawaiian dish starring seasoned fish. Gluten-free buckwheat is key in this Californian-style version.

Serves *4*

1 bunch spring onions, trimmed
1 tbs olive oil
⅓ cup (80ml) rice vinegar
1 garlic clove, crushed
1 tsp caster sugar
1 tbs tamari (gluten-free soy sauce)
200g buckwheat, cooked
   according to packet instructions
350g sashimi-grade salmon,
   cut into 1cm cubes
1 tsp sesame oil
4 baby (Dutch) carrots, very
   thinly sliced lengthways
Avocado wedges, snow pea
   sprouts, sliced nori, white sesame
   seeds and shichimi togarashi
   (Japanese 'seven-flavour' spice
   mix – from Asian food shops),
   to serve

Heat a chargrill pan over high heat. Drizzle spring onions with olive oil and add to pan. Cook, turning, for 5 minutes or until lightly charred.

Place vinegar, garlic, sugar and tamari in a bowl and stir until sugar dissolves. Add to buckwheat and toss to coat.

Divide buckwheat mixture among serving bowls. Toss salmon with sesame oil. Top buckwheat mixture with charred spring onions, salmon, carrot, avocado and snow pea sprouts. Sprinkle with nori, sesame seeds and shichimi togarashi to serve.

Kale, prosciutto & goat's cheese fritters with green goddess dressing

Kale isn't just for adding raw to salads or baking into chips – use it in fritters for a nutrient boost.

Serves *2*

½ bunch (about 150g) kale,
  stalks removed
150g soft goat's cheese, crumbled
4 slices prosciutto, chopped
4 spring onions, thinly sliced
⅔ cup (100g) plain flour
3 eggs, lightly beaten
1 long green chilli, finely chopped
2 tbs finely chopped flat-leaf
  parsley leaves
⅓ cup (80ml) extra virgin olive oil
Sliced cucumber, red vein sorrel
  leaves, podded broad beans,
  halved sugar snap peas, micro
  basil or small basil leaves and
  green goddess dressing (see
  recipe, p 116), to serve

Place kale in a heatproof bowl and cover with boiling water. Set aside for 2 minutes to soften. Drain and refresh under cold water. Finely chop and squeeze out excess water. Place in a bowl with goat's cheese, prosciutto, spring onion, flour, egg, chilli and parsley. Season with freshly ground black pepper.

Heat oil in a large non-stick frypan over medium heat. In 2 batches, add ⅓ cup mixture per fritter to frypan, flattening slightly with a spatula. Cook for 3-4 minutes each side or until golden and crisp. Remove from pan and drain on paper towel. Keep warm.

Divide fritters between serving plates. Add cucumber, sorrel, broad beans, sugar snap peas and basil. Season and serve with dressing.

L-R: Dan dan noodles with prawns (P 106)
Sriracha & lemongrass mussels (P 107)

Dan dan noodles with prawns

Dan dan noodles is a famous Sichuan street-food dish traditionally containing pork. Here it's made lighter by switching the meat for prawns and peanut butter for almond butter.

Serves *4*

1 tsp five-spice powder
1½ tbs chilli paste
2 tbs honey
1 tbs almond butter
2 tbs soy sauce
500g green prawns, peeled
   (tails intact), deveined
1 tbs sunflower oil
3cm piece (15g) ginger,
   finely chopped
2 spring onions, finely chopped,
   plus shredded spring onion
   to serve
2 garlic cloves, finely chopped
300g Chinese wheat noodles,
   cooked according to
   packet instructions
Toasted white sesame seeds,
   to serve

Dan dan sauce
2 tbs tahini
2 tbs soy sauce
2 tbs chilli oil
2 tbs rice vinegar

For the sauce, place all ingredients in a bowl. Gradually stir in 100ml warm water until combined. Set aside.

Place the five-spice, chilli paste, honey, almond butter and soy in a bowl and whisk until smooth. Add prawns and stir to coat.

Heat oil in a non-stick frypan over medium heat. Add ginger, spring onion and garlic, and cook, stirring, for 2-3 minutes or until softened. Transfer to a bowl. Add prawns to the pan in a single layer and cook, turning once, for 4-5 minutes or until cooked through. Return ginger mixture to the pan and toss to coat.

Toss noodles with the dan dan sauce and divide among serving bowls. Top with prawns, sesame seeds and shredded spring onion to serve.

Sriracha & lemongrass mussels

Sriracha is a Thai hot sauce made from chilli, vinegar, garlic, sugar and salt. Mix it with lemongrass and wine to supercharge mussels for a fast weeknight meal.

Serves *2*

80g unsalted butter, chopped
1 lemongrass stalk (inner core
   only), thick part coarsely grated,
   top stem reserved
2 tbs sriracha or chilli paste
150ml dry white wine
1kg pot-ready mussels
Coriander leaves and thickly
   sliced baguette, to serve

Place butter, grated lemongrass and stem, sriracha and wine in a large saucepan over medium-high heat and cook for 5 minutes or until wine has slightly reduced and butter has melted. Add mussels and cover with a lid. Cook, shaking the pan, for 3-4 minutes or until mussels have opened. Discard any closed mussels.

Divide mussels and cooking liquid between serving bowls. Sprinkle with coriander and serve immediately with bread.

Umami-rich miso transforms Italian bolognese, while brussels sprouts team with bacon for a veg-boosted carbonara.

Miso spaghetti bolognese

Serves *4-6*

2 tbs olive oil
1 onion, finely chopped
1 carrot, finely chopped
2 celery stalks, finely chopped
4 garlic cloves, finely chopped
1 small red chilli, finely chopped
1½ tsp fennel seeds
⅓ cup (105g) white (shiro) miso
2 tbs tomato paste
500g beef mince
2 x 400g cans chopped tomatoes
2 cups (500ml) beef stock
2 bay leaves
400g spaghetti, cooked according
  to packet instructions
Finely grated parmesan and
  basil leaves, to serve

Heat oil in a large, deep saucepan over medium heat. Add onion, carrot and celery, and cook, stirring, for 10 minutes or until softened. Add garlic and chilli, and cook, stirring, for 5 minutes or until fragrant. Add fennel seeds, miso and tomato paste, and cook, stirring, for a further 2 minutes or until vegetables are coated.

Add mince and cook, breaking up mince with a wooden spoon, for 10 minutes or until browned. Add tomato, stock and bay leaves, and bring to a simmer. Cook for 1 hour or until thickened and reduced. Season to taste (be careful as miso is salty).

Fold pasta through sauce and divide among serving bowls. Sprinkle with parmesan and basil leaves to serve.

No-egg carbonara with crispy brussels sprouts

Serves *4*

4 smoky bacon rashers, chopped
2 tbs extra virgin olive oil
50g unsalted butter, chopped
1 eschalot, finely chopped
500g brussels sprouts, blanched,
  refreshed, halved
1 cup (250ml) chicken stock
1¼ cups (100g) finely grated
  parmesan, plus extra to serve
300g linguine, cooked according
  to packet instructions

Place bacon in a large non-stick frypan over medium heat and cook slowly for 6-8 minutes or until fat is rendered. Remove bacon with a slotted spoon, reserving fat.

Add oil and 20g butter to pan and melt over medium-high heat. Add eschalot and cook, stirring occasionally, for 2 minutes or until softened. Add sprouts and cook, tossing, for 6-8 minutes or until caramelised. Add stock, remaining 30g butter and bacon, then bring to a rapid simmer. Remove from heat and stir in parmesan. Season with freshly ground black pepper.

Fold pasta through sauce, stirring well to combine. Divide among serving bowls. Sprinkle with extra parmesan and freshly ground black pepper to serve.

Pork, sage & white wine manicotti

The lesser-known cousin of cannelloni, manicotti are thin crepes that are stuffed, covered in sauce and baked. You can use store-bought dried cannelloni tubes for this recipe – just bake for an extra 25 minutes.

Serves *6-8*

⅓ cup (80ml) olive oil
1 onion, finely chopped
2 garlic cloves, finely chopped
1 carrot, finely chopped
1 celery stalk, finely chopped
750g pork mince
1 bunch sage, leaves picked
1 cup (250ml) white wine
1 cup (250ml) chicken stock
3 x 400g cans chopped tomatoes
1 cup (100g) finely grated
  mozzarella
Finely grated parmesan, to serve

Crepes
1½ cups (225g) plain flour
1 tbs thyme leaves
1½ cups (375ml) milk
2 eggs, lightly beaten
¼ cup (60ml) olive oil

For the crepe batter, place flour and thyme in a bowl with a pinch of salt flakes. Make a well in the centre and add milk and egg. Whisk to form a smooth batter. Set aside to rest.

Heat ¼ cup (60ml) oil in a large frypan over medium heat. Add onion, garlic, carrot and celery, and cook, stirring occasionally, for 10 minutes or until softened. Increase heat to high and add mince. Cook, breaking up mince with a wooden spoon, for 10 minutes or until browned. Tear half the sage leaves and add to pan with wine. Cook until wine has reduced by half. Stir through stock and 2 cans tomatoes. Reduce heat to medium and cook, stirring occasionally, for 30 minutes or until thick and reduced. Season.

Meanwhile, to cook the crepes, heat 1 tsp oil in a 22cm non-stick frypan. Add ½ cup (125ml) batter to the pan, swirling to coat the base. Cook for 1 minute or until golden, then flip and cook for a further minute or until just cooked. Remove from pan and set aside. Repeat with remaining oil and batter to make 12 crepes.

Preheat oven to 200°C. Place 1 crepe on a clean work surface and spoon about ½ cup pork mixture evenly along the bottom third. Roll up to form a fat cylinder. Place in a baking dish, seam-side down. Repeat with remaining crepes and pork mixture.

Pour over remaining 1 can tomatoes and scatter with mozzarella and remaining sage. Drizzle with remaining 1 tbs oil and season. Bake for 25 minutes or until golden and bubbling. Scatter with parmesan and serve immediately.

Charred T-bone with oyster sauce & mushroom butter

The simple addition of oyster sauce to much-loved mushroom butter gives midweek steak new appeal.

Serves *2*

1 tbs olive oil
800g T-bone steak
80g unsalted butter, chopped
1 tbs oyster sauce
200g Swiss brown mushrooms,
  larger mushrooms halved
150g chestnut mushrooms

Preheat oven to 200°C. Heat oil in a large frypan over medium-high heat. Season steak and add to pan. Cook, turning once, for 10 minutes or until browned all over. Transfer to a baking dish and roast for 7-8 minutes for medium-rare or until cooked to your liking. Cover loosely with foil and set aside for 10 minutes to rest.

Meanwhile, heat butter in a frypan over high heat. Add oyster sauce and stir to combine. Add mushrooms and cook, tossing, for 2-3 minutes or until golden. Pour sauce over steak and thickly slice to serve.

L-R: **Green goddess dressing** (P 116), **Salsa verde** (P 116),
Roasted tomato & parmesan dressing (P 116), **Veganaise – egg-free mayo** (P 117),
Roasted lemon dressing (P 117), **Chilli sesame sauce** (P 117)

Genius extras
Essential dressings

Clever combinations are all you need to add instant flavour to your favourite meals.

Green goddess dressing

Makes *1½ cups*

½ bunch each mint, flat-leaf
  parsley, dill and tarragon,
  leaves picked
Juice of ½ a lemon
½ cup (120g) sour cream
½ cup (140g) thick Greek-style
  yoghurt

Place all ingredients in a food processor, season and whiz until smooth. Transfer to a jar and chill for up to 5 days. Serve with fritters, roasted cauliflower or grilled chicken.

Salsa verde

Makes *1 cup*

1 bunch mint, leaves picked
¼ bunch basil, leaves picked
1 garlic clove, crushed
¼ cup (50g) capers in vinegar,
  drained
Juice of 1 lemon
⅓ cup (80ml) extra virgin olive oil

Place all ingredients in a food processor, season and whiz until smooth. Transfer to a jar and chill for up to 2 days. Serve with roasted lamb or chicken, or try it with our roasted pumpkin & honey prawn bruschetta (see recipe, p 192).

Roasted tomato & parmesan dressing

Makes *1½ cups*

500g tomatoes, roughly chopped
3 garlic cloves, unpeeled
60g parmesan, thickly sliced
½ cup (125ml) extra virgin olive oil
2 tbs red wine vinegar
2 tbs thyme leaves

Preheat the oven to 220°C. Line a baking tray with baking paper. Place tomato, garlic and parmesan on prepared tray and drizzle with 2 tbs oil. Season and roast for 30 minutes or until tomato has broken down. Cool slightly. Peel garlic and transfer mixture to a food processor with vinegar, thyme and remaining 85ml oil. Season and whiz until smooth. Transfer to a jar and chill for up to 3 days. Serve with a green bean and feta salad or a cold pasta salad, or lightly toss with salad greens.

Veganaise – egg-free mayo

Makes *1¼ cups*

300g packet silken tofu
2 tsp Dijon mustard
1 tbs white wine vinegar
1 small garlic clove, crushed
2 tbs extra virgin olive oil

Place tofu in a food processor and whiz until smooth. Add mustard, vinegar and garlic, and whiz to combine. With the motor running, add the oil in a thin, steady stream until thick and emulsified. Season with salt flakes. Transfer to a jar and chill for up to 3 days. Serve as a vegan alternative to mayonnaise with sweet potato fries or burgers, or use in our zucchini caesar salad dressing (see recipe, p 49).

Chilli sesame sauce

Makes *¾ cup*

2 tbs tahini
2 tbs soy sauce
2 tbs chilli oil
2 tbs rice vinegar

Place tahini, soy, oil and vinegar in a bowl and whisk to combine. Add 100ml warm water and whisk again to combine. Transfer to a jar and chill for up to 1 week. Serve with dumplings, Asian noodle dishes or grilled chicken.

Roasted lemon dressing

Makes *1 cup*

3 lemons, halved, seeds removed
150ml extra virgin olive oil
1 garlic clove, crushed

Preheat oven to 220°C. Arrange lemon halves, cut-side down, on a baking tray and drizzle with 50ml oil. Season. Roast for 35 minutes or until soft and juicy. Cool slightly, then using a lemon squeezer, squeeze out juice. Discard peel or roughly chop and add to dressing (depending how lemony you like it). Whisk in garlic and remaining 100ml oil, and season. Transfer to a jar and chill for up to 1 week. Serve with salad greens or roasted broccoli, or spoon over cooked prawns or fish.

Chapter Five

One-pot dinners

Let your cookware do the work with these fast-prep dishes that mean you can get out of the kitchen quick. Tender slow-cooked meat, the new speedy way to roast chicken and a no-layer lasagne that throws out the rule book are just the beginning. The best part? It's all taken care of in just one pot.

Butter chicken with chilli & cucumber salad and dill yoghurt

The secret ingredient to lighten up everyone's favourite Indian recipe is coconut milk instead of cream. The aromatic spice mix can be stored for up to four months, so make extra and keep this dish on high rotation.

Serves *4*

1 tbs olive oil
6 chicken thighs, bone in, skin on (ask your butcher)
¼ cup best chicken spice mix (see recipe, p 147)
1 onion, finely chopped
2 garlic cloves, finely chopped
4cm piece (20g) ginger, finely chopped
50g unsalted butter, chopped
1 tbs tandoori paste
2 tbs tomato paste
2 cups (500ml) chicken stock
400g can chopped tomatoes
½ cup (125ml) coconut milk
2 cups (560g) thick Greek-style yoghurt
½ cup dill fronds, roughly chopped, plus extra to serve
Juice of 1 lemon
2 green chillies, thinly sliced
1 telegraph cucumber, thinly sliced
Micro coriander (optional), roti and lime wedges, to serve

Heat oil in a large, deep saucepan over high heat. Season chicken and add to pan, skin-side down. Cook for 6 minutes or until golden, then turn and cook for a further 4 minutes or until sealed. Remove from pan and set aside.

Add the spice mix, onion, garlic, ginger and butter to the pan and reduce heat to low. Cook, stirring occasionally, for 5-6 minutes or until onion is softened. Add tandoori and tomato pastes, and cook for a further 1 minute or until pastes are heated through. Add stock and tomato.

Return chicken to pan, increase heat to high and bring to the boil.

Reduce heat to medium-low and cook, stirring occasionally, for 1 hour or until chicken is tender and sauce has reduced by half. Season, then remove from heat and stir in coconut milk.

Meanwhile, to make the dill yoghurt, combine yoghurt, dill and lemon juice in a bowl. Season and chill until needed.

Sprinkle curry with chilli, cucumber, extra dill and micro coriander, if using. Serve with roti, lime wedges and dill yoghurt.

Oven-roasted meatballs with kale pesto

Make it easy with fennel-spiked sausage meat and store-bought kale or basil pesto.

Serves *4*

500g pork and fennel sausages
1 egg, lightly beaten
200g fresh breadcrumbs
¼ cup (65g) kale pesto
   (from delis) or basil pesto
4 garlic cloves, finely chopped
1 bunch oregano, leaves picked
1 tbs olive oil
1 red onion, finely chopped
700ml tomato sugo
1 cup (100g) coarsely grated
   mozzarella
Basil leaves, to serve

Squeeze meat from sausage casings and combine in a bowl with egg, breadcrumbs, pesto and 1 chopped garlic clove. Roughly chop half the oregano and stir through mixture. Season. With slightly wet hands, roll mixture into 6cm balls. Place on a plate and chill for 30 minutes to firm up.

Preheat oven to 200°C. Heat oil in a deep ovenproof pan over medium heat. Add meatballs, in batches if necessary, and cook, turning, for 6-7 minutes or until browned all over. Remove from pan and set aside. Add the onion and remaining 3 chopped garlic cloves and cook, stirring, for 3 minutes or until onion is softened. Stir through sugo and remaining oregano. Season. Bring to a simmer.

Return meatballs to pan and scatter with mozzarella. Transfer to the oven and bake for 15-20 minutes or until meatballs are cooked through and cheese is bubbling. Season and scatter with basil to serve.

Six-spice chicken pilau (P 126)

Smoky fish pie with cauliflower and bacon (P 127)

Six-spice chicken pilau

Our take on a favourite Rick Stein recipe written for delicious. *in 2010, this wonderful winter warmer is loaded with fragrant spices.*

Serves *4*

50g ghee or unsalted butter
1kg chicken thigh fillets
2 onions, thinly sliced
5cm piece (25g) ginger,
   finely chopped
3 garlic cloves, finely chopped
⅓ cup fresh curry leaves, plus fried
   curry leaves (optional) to serve
1 tsp each ground cinnamon,
   ground turmeric and
   fennel seeds
2 tsp each chilli powder, cumin
   seeds and mustard seeds
2 cups (400g) basmati rice
3 cups (750ml) chicken stock
Coriander sprigs and coconut
   cream, to serve

Melt ghee in a large saucepan over medium heat. Season chicken and add to pan. Cook, turning once, for 6 minutes or until browned all over. Remove from pan and set aside.

Reduce heat to low. Add onion and a pinch of salt flakes to pan. Cook, stirring, for 10 minutes or until softened. Add ginger, garlic, curry leaves and spices, and cook, stirring, for 2 minutes or until fragrant. Add rice and stir to coat. Return chicken to pan, increase heat to medium and add stock. Bring to the boil. Reduce heat to low, cover with a lid and cook, without stirring, for 25 minutes or until liquid has been absorbed. Set aside, covered, for 10 minutes to finish cooking. Stir rice with a fork to separate grains.

Divide pilau between serving bowls. Scatter with coriander and fried curry leaves, if using. Serve with coconut cream.

Smoky fish pie with cauliflower and bacon

Serves *6-8*

5 (about 1kg) sebago potatoes,
   peeled, cut into 3cm pieces
50g unsalted butter, chopped
1⅓ cups (330ml) milk
1 tbs olive oil
2 leeks (white part only),
   thinly sliced
2 bacon rashers, finely chopped
2 garlic cloves, finely chopped
¼ small (about 250g) cauliflower,
   finely chopped
¼ cup thyme leaves
100g smoked trout, flaked
⅓ cup (50g) plain flour
1kg firm white skinless fish fillets
   (such as ling or blue-eye),
   cut into 6cm cubes
250g sour cream
Chopped dill, salad leaves
   and roasted lemon dressing
   (see recipe, p 117), to serve

Skip labour-intensive bechamel by tossing fish in flour and folding through sour cream. The result is a lighter, healthier fish pie with no sacrifice on flavour.

Preheat the oven to 200°C. Place potato in a large ovenproof pan and cover with cold salted water. Bring to the boil, then reduce heat to medium and cook for 15 minutes or until very tender. Drain and transfer to a bowl with butter and ⅔ cup (165ml) milk. Mash until smooth. Season and set aside.

Add oil and leek to pan and return to medium-low heat. Cook, stirring, for 6-8 minutes or until softened. Add bacon and cook for 5 minutes or until golden. Stir in garlic, cauliflower, thyme and trout. Season.

Place flour and fish in a bowl. Season and toss to coat. Add to cauliflower mixture. Stir in sour cream and remaining ⅔ cup (165ml) milk. Top mixture with mash and smooth the surface with the back of a spoon, swirling to create ridges. Transfer to the oven and bake for 50 minutes or until potato is golden. Set aside for 10 minutes to rest, then season and sprinkle with dill. Serve with salad leaves and roasted lemon dressing.

Herb-crusted salmon with sour cream tartare and sweet potato fries

Mixing ready-made dukkah with herbs is an easy way to season fish.

Serves *4*

1 large (about 800g) sweet potato,
  cut into 1cm-thick fries
2/3 cup (165ml) extra virgin olive oil
1½ cups (105g) fresh breadcrumbs
½ cup (60g) dukkah
1 bunch flat-leaf parsley,
  leaves picked, chopped
½ bunch dill, fronds picked,
  chopped
800g piece skinless salmon
  fillet, pin-boned

Sour cream tartare
1 cup (240g) sour cream
1 tsp Dijon mustard
½ small garlic clove, finely chopped
2 cornichons or gherkins,
  finely chopped
2 tsp capers in vinegar, drained,
  finely chopped
Finely grated zest and
  juice of ½ a lemon
2 tbs finely chopped flat-leaf
  parsley leaves
1 tsp finely chopped
  tarragon leaves

Preheat oven to 200°C. Grease a baking tray and line with baking paper. Toss sweet potato with 2 tbs oil. Season and arrange on prepared tray. Roast for 25 minutes or until tender. Transfer to a bowl and set aside.

Combine breadcrumbs, dukkah and herbs in a bowl with remaining ½ cup (125ml) oil. Place fish on the tray and coat with crumb mixture. Roast for 20 minutes for medium-rare or until cooked to your liking, adding fries to warm through during the last 5 minutes of cooking.

Meanwhile, for the tartare, combine all ingredients in a bowl. Chill until needed.

Serve fish with sour cream tartare and sweet potato fries.

L-R: Oregano & lemon roasted prawns with Greek salad (P 133)
Herb-crusted salmon with sour cream tartare and sweet potato fries (P 128)

Oregano & lemon roasted prawns with Greek salad

Make a midweek roast a reality with 10-minute honey and lemon prawns, the perfect sweet and sour combination.

Serves *4-6*

1kg large green prawns
Pared zest of 2 lemons,
  cut into thin strips
3 sprigs Greek oregano (from
  delis – substitute 2 tsp dried
  oregano leaves), plus extra
  2 sprigs, leaves picked, to serve
2 tsp runny honey
2 tbs extra virgin olive oil

Greek salad
200g feta, sliced
500g heirloom cherry
  tomatoes, halved
4 truss tomatoes, sliced
1 red onion, thinly sliced
1 telegraph cucumber, halved
  lengthways, chopped
½ cup (75g) pitted kalamata olives
⅓ cup (80ml) extra virgin olive oil
Juice of 1 lemon

Preheat the oven to 250°C. Line a baking tray with baking paper. Using a sharp knife, butterfly the prawns by cutting lengthways along the belly until they open out. Remove vein and discard. Arrange prawns, cut-side up, on prepared tray and scatter with lemon zest and oregano. Drizzle with honey and oil, and season. Transfer to the oven and bake for 6 minutes or until cooked through.

For the salad, place all ingredients in a bowl. Season and toss to combine. Sprinkle with extra oregano and serve with prawns.

Caramelised pork belly with sweet pea salad

Serves *6-8*
Begin this recipe 1 day ahead.

1.8kg piece boneless
   pork belly, skin on
2 tbs fennel seeds
4 garlic cloves
1 bunch thyme, leaves picked
2 tbs olive oil
10 eschalots, peeled
½ cup (125ml) chicken stock
½ cup (125ml) maple syrup
3 cups (360g) frozen peas,
   blanched, refreshed
200g runner beans,
   blanched, refreshed
1 cup loosely packed snow
   pea tendrils

Just when you thought crackling couldn't get any better... brushing the skin with maple syrup right at the end of cooking gives this pork a sticky, crunchy caramelised finish.

Using a sharp knife, score the pork belly skin at 1cm intervals without cutting into the meat. Place pork on a rack set over a roasting pan and pour over 2 cups (500ml) boiling water to open the incisions. Pat dry with paper towel and discard water.

To make the marinade, heat a frypan over high heat. Add fennel seeds and toast for 1-2 minutes or until fragrant. Using a mortar and pestle, pound toasted seeds, garlic, ¼ cup thyme leaves and oil to a coarse paste. Rub mixture into pork flesh only, then place pork, skin-side up, on a baking tray. Chill, uncovered, overnight.

Remove pork from fridge to come to room temperature. Preheat the oven to 220°C. Grease a large roasting pan. Arrange the eschalots and remaining thyme in prepared pan. Add pork, skin-side up, and rub 2 tsp salt flakes into the skin. Roast for 1 hour or until the skin is beginning to crisp.

Reduce oven to 160°C. Add stock to pan and roast for a further 1 hour 45 minutes or until meat is cooked through and crackling is crisp and golden. Remove from oven and brush with maple syrup. Return to oven for a further 10 minutes or until lightly caramelised.

Remove pork from pan and set aside for 15 minutes to rest. When ready to serve, toss peas, beans and snow pea tendrils with hot cooking juices. Carve pork and serve with pea salad and roasted eschalots.

Brown butter Dory with roasted broccoli and creme fraiche

Say goodbye to soggy broccoli! Roast it until charred for a smoky flavour and a crisp, caramelised texture.

Serves *4*

2 large heads broccoli,
   cut into florets
¼ cup (60ml) extra virgin olive oil
100g unsalted butter, chopped
2 tbs thyme leaves
2 garlic cloves, sliced
¼ cup (50g) capers in vinegar,
   drained
4 x 150g John Dory fillets
   (or other delicate white fish)
1 lemon, thinly sliced
²/₃ cup (160g) creme fraiche
Small mint leaves and micro mint
   (optional), to serve

Preheat oven to 200°C. Line a large baking tray with baking paper. Arrange broccoli on prepared tray, drizzle with oil and dot with butter. Season. Scatter with thyme, garlic and capers. Roast for 30 minutes or until lightly charred.

Remove tray from oven and add fish. Top with lemon slices. Season. Cover with a piece of baking paper and fold over the edges to enclose. Return to oven for 10-12 minutes or until fish is just cooked through.

Spread creme fraiche over serving plates. Top with fish and broccoli, and drizzle with brown butter mixture from the tray. Sprinkle with mint leaves and micro mint, if using, to serve.

Lamb shank, mozzarella & eggplant lasagne (P 140)

Fast roast chicken with lemon, chilli & brown rice stuffing (P 141)

Lamb shank, mozzarella & eggplant lasagne

Slow-cooked lamb shanks take lasagne from an everyday dish to a dinner-party star, while making it free-form means no need for bechamel or lengthy layering.

Serves *8*

2 tbs olive oil
4 lamb shanks
1 carrot, finely chopped
1 onion, finely chopped
1 celery stalk, finely chopped
3 garlic cloves, finely chopped
½ cup (125ml) red wine
1 parmesan rind
2 x 400g cans chopped tomatoes
1 tbs thyme leaves
2 bay leaves
1 eggplant, cut into
   5mm-thick slices
3 fresh lasagne sheets,
   cut into large pieces
3 x 200g buffalo mozzarella
   balls, torn

Heat oil in a large ovenproof pan over high heat. Season lamb and add to pan. Cook, turning, for 10 minutes or until browned all over. Remove from pan and set aside.

Reduce heat to medium. Add carrot, onion and celery to pan and cook, stirring, for 10 minutes or until golden and softened. Add garlic and cook, stirring, for 1 minute or until fragrant. Add wine and simmer for 2 minutes to deglaze pan. Add parmesan rind, tomato, thyme and bay leaves. Return shanks to pan. Add 400ml water and bring to the boil. Reduce heat to low, cover and cook for 3 hours or until lamb is tender.

Preheat oven to 200°C. Remove shanks from pan and set aside to cool slightly. Shred meat from bones and discard bones. Return meat to pan. Add eggplant and lasagne sheets, pushing pasta under the sauce to create rough layers. Top with mozzarella.

Transfer pan to a baking tray and bake for 50 minutes, covering with foil if cheese becomes too browned, or until golden and bubbling. Set aside for 10 minutes to rest before serving.

Fast roast chicken with lemon, chilli & brown rice stuffing

Chicken and rice is much more than just that in this cleverly convenient dish. Halving the chicken makes for faster cooking, too, so you can enjoy it any night of the week.

Serves *4*

1.2kg whole chicken, halved
1 cup (200g) brown rice, cooked
   according to packet instructions
6 anchovies in oil, drained,
   roughly chopped
1 tbs capers in vinegar, drained
Finely grated zest and juice
   of 1 lemon, plus lemon
   wedges to serve
2 garlic cloves, crushed
2 small red chillies, sliced
⅓ cup (80ml) extra virgin olive oil
⅓ bunch flat-leaf parsley,
   leaves picked, chopped

Preheat the oven to 220°C. Line a baking tray with baking paper. Using a sharp knife, make several 5mm-deep incisions in the thickest parts of the chicken to ensure even cooking.

Combine rice, anchovy, capers, lemon zest and juice, garlic and chilli in a bowl and season with freshly ground black pepper. Arrange in a mound on prepared tray and place chicken, cut-side down, on top. Season chicken and drizzle with oil. Roast for 40 minutes or until chicken is golden and cooked through. Set aside for 10 minutes to rest.

Arrange stuffing on a serving dish and fold through parsley. Serve with chicken and lemon wedges.

Braised Chinese beef ribs with black vinegar and ginger

Serves *6-8*

2 tbs olive oil
1.6kg (about 5-6) beef short ribs
8cm piece (40g) ginger,
  thinly sliced
1 garlic bulb, halved crossways
1 cup (250ml) Chinese black
  (chinkiang) vinegar
  (from Asian food shops)
1 cup (250ml) Chinese rice wine
  (shaohsing)
½ cup (125ml) light soy sauce
2 cups (500ml) beef stock
5 star anise
1 tsp dried chilli flakes
1 cup (250g) firmly packed
  brown sugar
Micro red shiso or coriander
  leaves, to serve

Put everything into a pan and come back to fall-off-the-bone beef – this is the ultimate set-and-forget recipe!

Heat oil in a large saucepan over medium-high heat. Season beef and add to pan. Cook, turning, for 15 minutes or until browned all over. Add ginger, garlic, vinegar, rice wine, soy, stock, star anise and chilli to the pan. Cover with a lid and bring to the boil. Reduce heat to medium-low and cook for 3 hours 30 minutes or until beef is tender.

Carefully remove ribs from pan and set aside. Discard half the cooking liquid. Return remaining liquid to high heat and add sugar, stirring to dissolve. Simmer rapidly for 30 minutes or until mixture is thickened and reduced.

Return ribs to pan and cook for 10 minutes or until warmed through. Sprinkle with shiso and serve.

Clockwise from left: Orange & coriander marinade (P 146),
Juniper & fennel salt rub (P 146), Smoky chipotle seasoning (P 146),
Ginger, chilli & golden syrup glaze (P 147),
Best chicken spice mix (P 147)

Genius extras
Marinades

*Add plenty of flavour
with these easy mixes.*

Orange & coriander marinade

Makes *⅔ cup*

6 garlic cloves
2 small red chillies, finely chopped
2 tbs each cumin, coriander
   and fennel seeds
½ tsp ground cinnamon
Finely grated zest and
   juice of 2 oranges

Using a mortar and pestle, pound garlic, chilli, spices and orange zest until roughly crushed. Stir in orange juice. Transfer to a jar and chill for up to 5 days. Use to marinate lamb shoulder or lamb ribs for the barbecue, or smaller poultry such as quail and spatchcock.

Juniper & fennel salt rub

Makes *¾ cup*

½ cup (40g) salt flakes
1 tbs each juniper berries, pepper
   berries and fennel seeds
½ tsp dried chilli flakes

Combine all ingredients in an airtight jar and store at room temperature for up to 6 months. Rub into the skin of pork belly for a flavoursome crackling.

Smoky chipotle seasoning

Makes *⅓ cup*

1 tbs smoked chipotle or
   smoked paprika (pimenton)
1 tbs coriander seeds,
   toasted, ground
1 tbs dried oregano
1 tsp garlic powder
2 tsp onion flakes

Combine all ingredients in an airtight jar and store at room temperature for up to 4 months. Use as a Mexican seasoning in tacos or braises, or dust over fish before baking.

Ginger, chilli & golden syrup glaze

Makes *½ cup*

5cm piece (25g) ginger,
  finely grated
3 garlic cloves, crushed
2 tbs finely chopped coriander root
2 tsp dried chilli flakes
½ cup (125ml) golden syrup

Combine all ingredients in a jar
and chill for up to 1 week. Use as
a marinade or glaze for chicken
wings, pork ribs or salmon.

Best chicken spice mix

Makes *½ cup*

3 tsp each ground cumin, ground
  ginger, ground coriander,
  smoked paprika (pimenton),
  ground turmeric and dried mint
3 tsp each fenugreek and caraway
  seeds, toasted, ground
¾ tsp each cardamom pods and
  cloves, toasted, roughly chopped

Combine all ingredients in an
airtight jar and store at room
temperature for up to 4 months.
Use to make butter chicken with
chilli & cucumber salad and dill
yoghurt (see recipe, p 120).

Chapter Six

Nourish every day

Strike the perfect balance every week with these nourishing recipes, where fresh produce and bright flavours take centre stage. Health-conscious eating goes from drab to delectable in nutrient-rich broths, wholesome soups and energising juices, which all have the added benefit of minimising waste in the kitchen.

Green miso with soba – two ways

Begin with an aromatic broth and heaps of vegetables, then finish with eggs or beef to make miso a nourishing meal. It's the new green soup.

Serves *4*

1 tbs olive oil
2 garlic cloves, crushed
3cm piece (15g) ginger,
   finely chopped
3 spring onions, thinly sliced
1/3 cup (105g) white (shiro) miso
1L (4 cups) chicken or
   vegetable stock
2 long green chillies, thinly sliced
270g soba noodles, cooked
   according to packet instructions
Sesame oil and nori komi furikake
   (Japanese rice seasoning – from
   Asian food shops), to serve

Vegetarian bowl option
1 bunch thin baby asparagus,
   trimmed
4 soft-boiled eggs, peeled,
   halved, to serve

Rare beef bowl option
1 tbs olive oil
2 x 200g sirloin steaks,
   at room temperature
1 tbs shichimi togarashi
   (Japanese 'seven-flavour' spice
   mix – from Asian food shops)
Amaranth leaves (optional), to serve

To make the miso broth base, heat oil in a large saucepan over medium-low heat. Add the garlic, ginger and spring onion, and cook, stirring, for 2-3 minutes or until softened and fragrant. Add miso, stock and chilli, increase heat to medium-high and bring to the boil.

For the vegetarian bowl, add asparagus to simmering broth base and cook for 2 minutes or until just tender. Divide noodles among serving bowls and spoon over miso broth. Top with boiled egg, drizzle with sesame oil, sprinkle with furikake, and serve.

For the rare beef bowl, heat oil in a non-stick frypan over medium-high heat. Season the beef and cook for 6 minutes, turning halfway, for medium-rare or until cooked to your liking. Scatter shichimi togarashi on a tray and coat cooked beef in spice. Cover loosely with foil and set aside for 5 minutes to rest.

Divide noodles among serving bowls and spoon over miso broth. Slice beef and add to bowls. Drizzle with sesame oil, sprinkle with furikake and amaranth leaves, if using, and serve.

Chilli, tomato & chorizo ribollita

A spicy twist on classic ribollita – an Italian bread soup fashioned from leftovers to minimise waste. Try adding borlotti or cannellini beans if you have them in the pantry.

Serves *4*

2 fresh chorizo sausages, casings removed, crumbled
1 fennel bulb, finely chopped
1 onion, finely chopped
1 carrot, finely chopped
1 celery stalk, finely chopped
2 garlic cloves, crushed
2 bay leaves
1 sprig rosemary, leaves picked
2 long red chillies, thinly sliced
2 x 400g cans chopped tomatoes
1L (4 cups) chicken stock
1 parmesan rind
4 slices day-old sourdough, toasted, torn
Baby kale, baby basil, buffalo mozzarella and dried chilli flakes, to serve

Place chorizo in a large saucepan over medium heat and cook, stirring, for 10 minutes or until browned. Remove half the chorizo and set aside.

Add fennel, onion, carrot and celery to the pan. Cook, stirring, for 10 minutes or until softened. Add garlic, bay leaves, rosemary, chilli, tomato, stock and parmesan rind. Bring to a simmer and cook for 30 minutes or until thickened and reduced. Discard parmesan rind and season.

Divide sourdough among bowls and top with soup, kale, basil and mozzarella. Sprinkle with chilli flakes and reserved chorizo, and serve.

Chicken & bay master stock (P 158)

L-R: **Nourishing chicken pho** (P 158)
Chickpea, bacon & chicken soup (P 159)
Spicy chicken & lentil harira (P 159)

This fragrant master stock is an excellent soup base or beautiful as a simple broth on its own. For a basic chicken noodle soup, return the shredded chicken to the pan and add noodles. Stir through baby spinach leaves and serve sprinkled with extra grated parmesan and lemon zest. For Asian soups, omit the parmesan and add extra aromatics.

Chicken & bay master stock

Makes *2L*

2 each carrots, onions and leeks
 (white part only), chopped
1 tbs olive oil
1.6kg whole chicken, rinsed, dried
2 celery stalks, chopped
6 bay leaves
1 thyme sprig
1 parmesan rind
Finely grated zest and
 juice of 1 lemon

Preheat the oven to 200°C. Place carrot, onion and leek on a baking tray and drizzle with oil. Roast for 30 minutes or until light golden. Transfer to a large stockpot.

Add chicken to pot with celery, bay leaves, thyme, parmesan rind and 3L (12 cups) water. Bring to the boil over high heat, then reduce heat to low and simmer for 1 hour 30 minutes or until chicken is cooked through and broth is rich.

Remove chicken from broth and set aside until cool enough to handle. Shred meat, discarding skin and bones, and reserve for another use or add back into stock. Discard parmesan rind and bay leaves. Stir through lemon zest and juice, and season.

Nourishing chicken pho

Serves *4-6*

2L (8 cups) chicken and bay
 master stock (made without
 parmesan rind – see recipe, left)
1 lemongrass stalk, bruised
5cm piece (25g) ginger, thinly sliced
4 star anise
4 kaffir lime leaves
1 long red chilli, thinly sliced
⅓ cup (80ml) fish sauce
Juice of 2 limes
3 tsp caster sugar
200g dried rice noodles, cooked
 according to packet instructions
Bean sprouts and thinly sliced
 spring onion, to serve
Mint, Thai basil and coriander
 leaves, to serve

Prepare the stock, but instead of shredding the meat, cut chicken into 4 pieces. Remove skin and carve meat into slices, discarding bones. Keep warm.

Strain stock into a bowl, discarding vegetables, then return stock to pan. Add lemongrass, ginger, star anise, kaffir lime leaves and chilli. Place over medium heat and bring to a simmer. Cook for 25 minutes or until fragrant and infused. Stir through fish sauce, lime juice and sugar. Adjust seasoning, if necessary.

Divide noodles among serving bowls and top with stock. Add sliced chicken, bean sprouts and spring onion. Sprinkle with herbs and serve.

Chickpea, bacon & chicken soup

Serves *4*

1.5L (6 cups) chicken and
  bay master stock
  (see recipe, opposite)
8 smoky bacon rashers,
  finely chopped
4 garlic cloves, finely chopped
3 rosemary sprigs, leaves picked,
  finely chopped
400g can chickpeas, rinsed, drained
150g cavatelli or baby shell pasta,
  cooked according to
  packet instructions
Shaved parmesan, to serve

Prepare the stock and strain into
a bowl, discarding vegetables.
Shred the meat, discarding skin
and bones, and set aside.

Place bacon in a heavy-based
saucepan over medium heat. Cook,
stirring occasionally, for 7-8 minutes
or until fat has rendered. Add garlic
and half the rosemary. Cook, stirring,
for 2 minutes or until fragrant. Add
chickpeas and stock, and bring
to a simmer. Cook for 20 minutes
or until chickpeas are soft and
liquid is reduced.

Remove about one-quarter of the
chickpeas and 2 cups (500ml) stock.
Using a stick blender or small food
processor, blend until smooth. Return
chickpea puree to pan, season and
stir to combine. Stir through pasta
and shredded chicken.

Divide soup among serving
bowls and sprinkle with parmesan
and remaining rosemary to serve.

Spicy chicken & lentil harira

Serves *4-6*

2L (8 cups) chicken and
  bay master stock
  (see recipe, opposite)
1 red onion, roughly chopped
1 red capsicum, roasted,
  peeled, seeds removed
8 vine-ripened tomatoes
2 garlic cloves, finely chopped
1 tbs harissa
1 tbs tomato paste
1 tsp each ground cumin,
  coriander and turmeric
400g can brown lentils,
  rinsed, drained
Roasted cherry tomatoes on
  the vine, zaatar and micro
  coriander (optional), to serve

Prepare the stock and strain into
a bowl, discarding vegetables.
Shred the meat, discarding skin
and bones, and set aside.

Place onion, capsicum, tomatoes,
garlic, harissa, tomato paste and
spices in a food processor and whiz
until combined. Transfer to a large
saucepan over low heat and cook,
stirring, for 10 minutes or until
fragrant. Add stock and lentils,
and cook for 30 minutes or until
thick and reduced. Stir through
shredded chicken and season.

Divide soup among serving
bowls and top with roasted cherry
tomatoes. Sprinkle with zaatar and
micro coriander, if using, to serve.

Carrot soup with sage & walnut brown butter

This fast, thrifty soup uses unpeeled carrots, retaining more of the vegetable's nutrients.

Serves *4*

160g unsalted butter
1 tbs olive oil
1 leek (white part only),
  thinly sliced
1kg carrots, chopped
4 thyme sprigs, leaves picked
1.25L (5 cups) chicken or
  vegetable stock
1 parmesan rind
½ cup (50g) walnuts, chopped
½ bunch sage, leaves picked

Melt 60g butter with oil in a large saucepan over medium heat. Add leek and cook, stirring occasionally, for 8 minutes or until soft. Add carrot and thyme, and stir to coat. Cover, reduce heat to medium-low and cook for 8 minutes or until just tender. Remove lid, add stock and parmesan rind, and bring to a simmer. Cook for 25 minutes or until carrot is very soft. Remove from heat. Discard parmesan rind and use a stick blender to blend soup until smooth. Season.

Place remaining 100g butter in a frypan over medium heat and cook, shaking the pan, for 2 minutes or until melted. Add walnuts and cook, stirring, for 3 minutes or until nuts are toasted and butter is brown. Add sage and cook for a further minute or until crisp.

Divide soup among serving bowls and drizzle with brown butter mixture to serve.

Broccoli, lemon & feta soup with pistachio gremolata

Serves *4*

2 tbs olive oil
1 leek (white part only),
   finely chopped
3 garlic cloves, crushed
1 head broccoli, cut into
   small florets
100g baby spinach leaves
2 tbs chopped parsley stalks,
   plus ½ cup loosely packed leaves
1L (4 cups) chicken stock
Finely grated zest and
   juice of ½ a lemon
⅓ cup (55g) pistachios, chopped
2 tbs extra virgin olive oil
100g feta, crumbled
Watercress sprigs, to serve

If it's cold outside, substitute your green juice for a green soup. This cleansing bowlful can be made with any leftover greens, so give your crisper a clean-out.

Heat olive oil in a saucepan over low heat. Add leek and cook, stirring, for 10 minutes or until softened. Add two-thirds garlic, broccoli, spinach, parsley stalk and stock. Increase heat to high and bring to the boil. Cook for 10 minutes or until broccoli is tender. Stir through lemon juice and season. Remove from heat, add half the parsley leaves, and blend until smooth.

Combine lemon zest, pistachios, extra virgin olive oil and remaining garlic in a bowl. Roughly chop remaining ¼ cup parsley leaves and stir through mixture. Season with salt.

Divide soup among serving bowls and scatter with feta and watercress. Sprinkle with gremolata to serve.

Hot and sour tom yum is one of Thailand's greatest exports. A healthy, aromatic stock base is faster and simpler than you'd think, so give these two soups a go instead of ordering in.

Fast tom yum

Serves *4*

1 tbs coconut oil
2 lemongrass stalks, bruised
5cm piece (25g) ginger, thinly sliced
2 garlic cloves, bruised
4 kaffir lime leaves
1.5L (6 cups) chicken or fish stock
6 small red chillies,
    halved lengthways
1 tbs chilli paste
250g vine-ripened cherry tomatoes
150g oyster mushrooms,
    torn in half if large
500g green prawns, peeled
    (tails intact), deveined
Juice of 2 limes
¼ cup (60ml) fish sauce
3 tsp coconut sugar or brown sugar
270g somen noodles, cooked
    according to packet instructions

Heat oil in a large saucepan over medium heat. Add lemongrass, ginger and garlic, and cook for 30 seconds or until fragrant. Add kaffir lime leaves and stock, increase heat to medium-high and bring to the boil. Add chilli and chilli paste, and simmer for 5 minutes or until fragrant. Add tomatoes and mushrooms, and cook for 5 minutes or until tender. Add prawns and simmer for 2 minutes or until cooked through. Stir through lime juice, fish sauce and sugar.

Divide noodles among serving bowls. Add soup and serve.

Tom yum khaa

Serves *4*

1 tbs coconut oil
4 chicken thigh fillets
2 lemongrass stalks, bruised
5cm piece (25g) ginger, thinly sliced
2 garlic cloves, bruised
4 kaffir lime leaves
1L (4 cups) chicken stock
6 small red chillies, chopped
1 tbs chilli paste
1 bunch snake beans, halved
Juice of 2 limes
¼ cup (60ml) fish sauce
3 tsp coconut sugar or brown sugar
400ml coconut milk
Sunflower oil, to shallow-fry
15cm fresh lotus root (from Asian
    food shops), thinly sliced

Heat coconut oil in a large saucepan over medium heat. Season chicken and add to pan. Cook, turning, for 6 minutes or until golden. Set aside.

Add lemongrass, ginger and garlic to the pan and cook for 30 seconds or until fragrant. Add kaffir lime leaves and stock. Bring to the boil. Add chilli and chilli paste. Return chicken to pan. Simmer for 20 minutes or until cooked, then shred with 2 forks. Add beans and cook for 5 minutes or until tender. Add lime juice, fish sauce, sugar and coconut milk. Simmer for 5 minutes.

To make lotus chips, heat 1cm sunflower oil in a frypan over high heat. Add lotus root and cook for 1 minute, turning once, or until crisp.

Divide soup among serving bowls and serve with lotus chips.

L-R: Carrot, turmeric & miso juice (P 168)
Kombucha, celery & watermelon juice (P 168)
Beetroot, apple & lemon thyme juice (P 169)
Kale, avocado & parsley juice (P 169)

Genius extras
Wellness juices

WELLNESS JUICES

Boost your superfood quota and drink your vegies with these energising juices. With the added powers of apple cider vinegar, miso, kombucha, aloe vera or turmeric, they're good for your gut and rich in vitamins and antioxidants.

Carrot, turmeric & miso juice

Serves *2*

6 carrots
3 oranges, peeled, halved, plus orange slices to serve
10cm piece (50g) ginger
4cm piece (10g) turmeric
1 lemon, peeled
3 tsp white (shiro) miso

Push carrot, orange, ginger, turmeric and lemon through a juicer. Loosen miso with a little juice, then stir through remaining mixture. Fill serving glasses with ice cubes. Pour over juice and serve with orange slices.

Kombucha, celery & watermelon juice

Serves *2*
Begin this recipe 1 day ahead if making ice cubes.

Seeds of 2 pomegranates, plus extra seeds of 1 pomegranate for ice cubes (optional)
500g watermelon, rind removed, chopped into chunks
3 celery stalks, leaves attached, plus extra leaves to serve
200ml kombucha (from selected supermarkets and health food shops)

To make the pomegranate ice cubes, if using, sprinkle seeds of 1 pomegranate into an ice cube tray. Top with water and freeze overnight or until frozen.
   To make the juice, push the watermelon, pomegranate seeds and celery through a juicer. Add pomegranate ice cubes, if using, to serving glasses. Pour over juice and top with kombucha. Serve with extra celery leaves.

Beetroot, apple & lemon thyme juice

Serves *2*

2 large beetroot, peeled
4 Pink Lady apples
1 bunch mint, leaves picked
4cm piece (20g) ginger
2 limes, peeled
½ bunch lemon thyme, leaves
 picked, plus extra leaves to serve
½ cup (125ml) aloe vera juice
 (from health food shops)

Push beetroot, apples, mint, ginger, limes and lemon thyme through a juicer. Stir through aloe vera juice. Fill serving glasses with ice cubes. Pour over juice and serve with extra thyme leaves.

Kale, avocado & parsley juice

Serves *2*
Begin this recipe 1 day ahead if making ice cubes.

1 tbs chlorophyll (optional
 – from health food shops)
1 lime, thinly sliced (optional)
6 large kale leaves, stalks removed
1 avocado, stone removed, peeled
½ bunch celery
½ small bunch flat-leaf parsley,
 leaves picked
¼ cup (60ml) organic apple
 cider vinegar
Salt flakes, to serve

To make the chlorophyll ice cubes, if using, combine chlorophyll with 2 cups (500ml) water. Pour into ice cube trays and freeze overnight or until frozen.
 To make the dried lime slices, if using, preheat oven to 90°C. Line a baking tray with baking paper. Arrange lime slices on prepared tray in a single layer. Bake for 2 hours or until dry. Cool.
 To make the juice, push kale through a juicer, followed by avocado, celery and parsley. Stir through vinegar.
 Lightly rim serving glasses with salt and fill with chlorophyll ice cubes, if using. Pour over juice and serve with dried lime slices, if using.

Chapter Seven

Bring a plate

Next time someone asks you to bring a plate, rise to the occasion. This chapter has every solution to take an ordinary platter to an extraordinary centrepiece, reinventing potato salad, sticky wings, skewers and even garlic bread, plus tips on how to create the perfect cheese board. Make your next plate the talk of the party!

Caraway honey carrots with minted ricotta

Looking to move past carrot and dip? Elevate your dinner party status and update your roast vegetable repertoire with caramelised carrots and minty ricotta.

Serves 6

2 bunches baby (Dutch) carrots, blanched, refreshed
2 bacon rashers, finely chopped
1 tbs caraway seeds
¼ cup (60ml) runny honey
⅓ cup (80ml) extra virgin olive oil
Micro mint (optional), to serve

Minted ricotta
350g fresh ricotta
100g feta
Juice of ½ a lemon
¼ cup mint leaves, plus extra small mint leaves to serve

Peel and trim carrots, keeping about 10cm of the tops intact. Set aside. Place bacon in a non-stick frypan over low heat and cook, stirring, for 8 minutes or until crisp and golden. Add caraway seeds and cook, stirring, for 1 minute or until fragrant. Add honey and oil, and cook for 2 minutes or until heated through. Add carrots and cook, shaking the pan gently, for 5 minutes or until lightly caramelised.

Meanwhile, for the minted ricotta, place ricotta, feta, lemon juice and mint in a food processor and whiz to combine. Season.

To serve, spread minted ricotta over a serving plate and arrange carrots on top. Drizzle with honey mixture and scatter with extra mint leaves and micro mint, if using.

Put down the Tabasco sauce and lemon, and refresh your go-to oyster toppings.

Plum & eschalot mignonette

For *2 dozen oysters*

½ plum, finely chopped
½ small eschalot, finely chopped
¼ cup (60ml) red wine vinegar
1½ tsp freshly ground black pepper

Combine plum, eschalot, vinegar and pepper in a bowl and serve with oysters.

Pomegranate, sumac and creme fraiche

For *2 dozen oysters*

Seeds of ½ pomegranate
½ tsp sumac
Juice of 1 lemon
⅓ cup (80g) creme fraiche

Combine pomegranate seeds, sumac and lemon juice in a bowl. Spoon teaspoons of creme fraiche over oysters and top with dressing. Serve immediately.

Green chilli nam jim

For *2 dozen oysters*

1 small green chilli, finely chopped
½ tsp finely grated ginger
Juice of 1 lime
2 tsp fish sauce
2 tsp brown sugar
Micro coriander (optional), to serve

Combine chilli, ginger, lime juice, fish sauce and sugar in a small bowl and stir until sugar dissolves. Spoon over oysters and serve with micro coriander, if using.

Grilled eggplant and prosciutto with smoked almonds (P 179)

Lemon, radish, zucchini & feta salad (P 179)

Modernise your antipasti platter with a tangy shallot vinaigrette and smoked almonds, or reinvent the garden salad with a creamy roasted lemon dressing. Both of these dishes can be prepared ahead of time, then dressed when you're ready to serve.

Grilled eggplant and prosciutto with smoked almonds

Serves 6-8

3 eggplants, cut into
  5mm-thick slices
½ cup (125ml) extra virgin olive oil
3 spring onions, thinly sliced
2 tbs white wine vinegar
200g Sicilian olives, pitted
10 thin slices prosciutto
⅓ cup (55g) smoked almonds,
  roughly chopped

Preheat a barbecue or chargrill pan to high heat. Brush eggplant with 1 tbs oil and season. Add to grill and cook for 8 minutes, turning once, or until tender and grill marks appear.

Heat remaining 105ml oil in a small saucepan over low heat. Add spring onion and cook, stirring occasionally, for 3-4 minutes or until fragrant and softened. Stir through vinegar and season. Add olives and stir to coat.

Arrange eggplant on a serving platter. Top with prosciutto and almonds. Drizzle with spring onion dressing and serve.

Lemon, radish, zucchini & feta salad

Serves 4

1 eschalot, finely chopped
1 tsp sumac
2 bunches mixed radishes,
  trimmed, thinly sliced
1 zucchini, thinly sliced
½ bunch each flat-leaf parsley
  and mint, leaves picked
150g feta, thinly sliced
50g parmesan, shaved

Roasted lemon dressing
3 lemons, halved, seeds removed
150ml extra virgin olive oil
1 garlic clove, crushed

For the dressing, preheat oven to 220°C. Arrange lemon halves, cut-side down, on a baking tray and drizzle with 50ml oil. Season. Roast for 35 minutes, turning halfway, or until soft and juicy. Cool slightly, then use a lemon squeezer to juice. Discard lemon peel. Whisk in garlic and remaining 100ml oil. Season with salt flakes and freshly ground black pepper. Set aside until ready to serve or chill for up to 1 week.

Combine eschalot in a bowl with sumac and dressing. Set aside for 5 minutes to macerate.

Place radish, zucchini, herbs and cheeses in a large bowl and toss to combine. Add dressing mixture and toss to coat. Transfer to a platter and serve.

Kingfish sashimi with sake soy and crispy ginger

Seasoned seaweed and a light sake dressing are all that's needed with beautifully fresh sashimi-grade kingfish.

Serves 6

10cm piece (50g) young ginger, peeled
2 tbs vegetable oil
⅓ cup (80ml) sake
2 tbs light soy
1 tbs mirin
1 tbs lime juice
1 tsp caster sugar
500g sashimi-grade kingfish, thinly sliced
⅓ cup seasoned shredded sesame seaweed (from Asian food shops) or toasted nori sheets, shredded
10cm piece daikon (white radish – from Asian food shops), peeled, finely shredded
Micro red shiso, to serve

Finely shred ginger and pat dry with paper towel. Heat oil in a small frypan over medium-high heat. Add ginger and cook, stirring frequently, for 2-3 minutes or until crisp and golden. Remove and drain on paper towel. Set aside.

Place the sake, soy, mirin, lime juice and sugar in a bowl and stir until sugar dissolves. Arrange kingfish on a serving platter. Top with shredded seaweed, daikon, shiso and fried ginger. Serve with sake soy dressing.

Maple caramel pork belly skewers (P184)

Spiced marinated beetroot with preserved lemon & anchovy salsa (P 185)

Maple caramel pork belly skewers

Maple syrup is the secret ingredient in this Asian-style caramel, putting a flavoursome twist on sweet and sour pork.

Makes *15 skewers*

1 cup (250ml) maple syrup
1 tbs black peppercorns
2 garlic cloves, finely chopped
⅓ cup (80ml) fish sauce
Juice of 3 limes, plus
    lime cheeks to serve
1.5kg pork belly, skin removed,
    cut into 2cm cubes
⅓ cup (50g) toasted cashews,
    roughly chopped

Place the maple syrup, peppercorns, garlic, fish sauce and lime juice in a small saucepan over medium heat. Cook, stirring occasionally, for 30 minutes or until reduced by two-thirds. Preheat the oven or a flat barbecue plate to 200°C.

Thread pork onto metal skewers and brush liberally with maple caramel. Add to oven or barbecue and cook, turning and brushing with caramel every 10 minutes, for 45 minutes or until sticky and caramelised.

Arrange pork skewers on a serving platter. Scatter with cashews and serve with lime cheeks.

Spiced marinated beetroot with preserved lemon & anchovy salsa

Skip the canned beetroot and opt for a mix of fresh young beets pickled in a fragrant spiced dressing at your next barbecue.

Serves *4-6*

1 tbs coriander seeds
1 bunch each red and gold
  baby beetroot, trimmed
1 preserved lemon quarter
  (from delis), flesh and white pith
  removed, rind finely chopped
4 anchovies in oil, drained,
  finely chopped
1 eschalot, finely chopped
2 tsp dried chilli flakes
1/3 cup (80ml) rice wine vinegar
1/3 cup (80ml) extra virgin olive oil
2 x 125g balls buffalo
  mozzarella, torn
Toasted sliced baguette and
  micro basil (optional), to serve

Place coriander seeds in a small frypan over low heat and toast, shaking the pan, for 3 minutes or until fragrant. Using a mortar and pestle, roughly crush. Set aside.

Enclose each beetroot in microwave-safe plastic wrap and microwave for 10 minutes or until tender (alternatively, steam until tender). Remove from plastic wrap, allow to cool slightly, then peel and discard skins. Halve any larger beetroot.

Place preserved lemon, anchovy, eschalot, chilli, vinegar, oil and crushed coriander seeds in a bowl and stir to combine. Season. Add gold beetroot and stir to coat. Set aside for 5 minutes to marinate.

Drain gold beetroot, reserving dressing. Arrange red and gold beetroot on a serving platter. Add mozzarella and baguette slices. Drizzle with dressing and scatter with micro basil, if using, to serve.

L-R: Peach, currant & maple chutney (P 188)
Soft quince, vermouth & rosemary paste (P 188)

Cheeses (clockwise from top left): burrata, Delice des Deux-Sevres, Le Chabichou d'Antan, Challerhocker, Saint Simeon, Cashel Irish blue

Impress with your next cheese board by making your own condiments. To sterilise jars, wash glass jars and metal lids in hot, soapy water, then rinse and dry. Place on a baking tray in a 120°C oven for 20 minutes. Carefully remove and fill jars, and seal while they are still hot.

A range of textures, milks and maturities will balance your cheese selection. Try:

Burrata
Fresh cow's milk cheese stuffed with stracciatella and cream.

Cashel Irish blue
A ripe semi-soft farmhouse cheese.

Challerhocker
A nutty aged Swiss cheese washed in spices and brine.

Delice des Deux-Sevres
A French goat's cheese with a unique salted charcoal finish.

Le Chabichou d'Antan
A tangy and chalky goat's cheese.

Saint Simeon
An oozy, creamy French brie coated in a delicate white mould.

Peach, currant & maple chutney

Makes *2 x 500ml jars*

5cm piece (25g) ginger, finely chopped
1 cup (250ml) verjuice or white wine
1 cup (250ml) maple syrup
1 cup (250ml) organic apple cider vinegar
½ cup (75g) currants
2 tsp dried chilli flakes
6 large (about 1.5kg) peaches, stones removed, roughly chopped

Place ginger, verjuice, maple syrup and vinegar in a large saucepan over medium-high heat. Bring to a simmer and add currants, chilli and peach. Stir to combine. Cook, uncovered, stirring occasionally, for 1 hour or until the liquid has almost completely reduced and the mixture is thick and jammy.

Divide hot chutney between two 500ml sterilised jars and cover with fitted lids. Invert jars to create a sterile seal. Use immediately or store, unopened, in a cool, dry place for up to 6 months. Once opened, the chutney will keep chilled for up to 3 months.

Soft quince, vermouth & rosemary paste

Makes *750ml jar*

6 large (about 2kg) quinces
Juice of ½ a lemon
2½ cups (550g) caster sugar
2 sprigs each rosemary, sage and bay leaves
2⅓ cups (580ml) dry vermouth
2 tsp pink or black peppercorns

Peel quinces and cut into eighths, removing the hard core. Place in a bowl of cold water with the lemon juice. Set aside until ready to use.

Place the sugar, half the herbs, 2 cups (500ml) vermouth, peppercorns and 1L (4 cups) water in a large saucepan over medium heat. Cook, stirring, for 10 minutes or until sugar dissolves. Drain quince, add to pan and stir to combine. Reduce heat to low. Cover the surface with a round of baking paper and cook, stirring occasionally, for 4 hours or until deep pink and reduced, adding remaining herbs for the last 30 minutes.

Cool slightly, then stir in the remaining ⅓ cup (80ml) vermouth. Remove herb sprigs. Spoon into a 750ml sterilised jar, cover with a fitted lid and invert jar to create a sterile seal. Use immediately or store, unopened, in a cool, dry place for up to 1 year. Once opened, the quince paste will keep chilled for up to 6 months.

Sticky chilli bean paste chicken wings

Chilli bean paste is a Chinese condiment that adds fast flavour to these wings. Marinate for up to three days ahead, ready to roast for a party.

Serves *6-8*

1.4 kg chicken wings
⅓ cup (100g) chilli bean paste
   (from Asian food shops)
   or hot chilli condiment
¼ cup whole dried chillies
⅓ cup (80ml) runny honey
⅓ cup (80ml) Chinese rice wine
   (shaohsing) or dry sherry
2 tbs light soy sauce
⅓ cup (50g) roasted salted
   peanuts, chopped
Micro coriander (optional), to serve

Preheat the oven to 220°C. Line a baking tray with baking paper. Place chicken in a large bowl with chilli bean paste, dried chillies, honey, rice wine and soy, and toss to coat. Arrange on prepared tray in a single layer. Bake, basting with marinade every 15 minutes, for 50 minutes or until golden and caramelised.

Arrange chicken on a large serving platter and scatter with peanuts and micro coriander, if using. Serve hot or at room temperature.

Roasted pumpkin & honey prawn bruschetta

Give standard tomato and basil bruschetta a break and try silky charred pumpkin with sweet honey prawns instead.

Serves *8*

1kg Jap pumpkin, seeds removed, cut into wedges
1/3 cup (80ml) extra virgin olive oil
1/2 tsp dried chilli flakes
2 1/2 tsp smoked paprika (pimenton)
1/3 cup (80ml) runny honey
1 garlic clove, crushed
2 tbs olive oil
16 large green prawns, peeled (tails intact), deveined
8 slices sourdough, toasted
1/2 cup (120g) sour cream
Salsa verde (see recipe, p 116) and micro basil (optional), to serve

Preheat the oven to 220°C. Line a baking tray with baking paper. Arrange pumpkin in a single layer on prepared tray. Drizzle with extra virgin olive oil and scatter with chilli and 1/2 tsp paprika. Roast for 1 hour or until tender and caramelised. Set aside to cool.

Meanwhile, combine honey, garlic, olive oil and remaining 2 tsp paprika in a bowl. Add the prawns and toss to coat. Set aside for 15 minutes to marinate.

When ready to serve, arrange sourdough on a serving platter. Scoop pumpkin flesh from skin and spread over sourdough, then dollop with sour cream. Heat a large non-stick frypan over medium heat. Season prawns and add to pan. Cook, turning once, for 6-7 minutes or until caramelised.

Top bruschetta with prawns, drizzle with salsa verde and scatter with micro basil, if using, to serve.

Garlic bread and potato salad will never disappear from menus – thankfully! But have a go at reworking these classics with fresh herbs and zesty flavours.

Sage, thyme & garlic bread

Serves *8-10*

1 baguette
150g unsalted butter, chopped, softened
4 garlic cloves, crushed
½ bunch each sage and thyme, leaves picked
Finely grated parmesan, to serve

Preheat the oven to 200°C. Line a baking tray with baking paper. Cut the loaf at 1cm intervals, being careful not to cut all the way through. Place on prepared tray.

Combine butter and garlic in a bowl, season and spread between slices. Stuff with herbs. Cover loaf with foil and bake for 20 minutes or until golden, then remove foil and bake for a further 5 minutes or until crusty. Cool slightly, then sprinkle with parmesan and serve.

Potato salad with macadamia & dill pesto

Serves *6-8*

1kg kipfler potatoes, scrubbed
⅓ cup (80ml) extra virgin olive oil
1 cup (70g) sourdough breadcrumbs
Finely grated zest of 1 lemon
6 slices round pancetta
2 cups watercress, leaves picked

Macadamia & dill pesto
½ cup (75g) toasted macadamias
1 bunch dill, fronds picked
1 bunch flat-leaf parsley, leaves picked
⅓ cup (25g) finely grated parmesan
Finely grated zest and juice of 1 lemon
½ cup (125ml) extra virgin olive oil
1 garlic clove, crushed

For the pesto, whiz all ingredients in a food processor. Season and chill.

Place potatoes in a saucepan and cover with cold water. Bring to the boil. Reduce heat to medium-low and cook for 15 minutes or until tender. Drain and refresh. Cut into large pieces and place in a bowl.

Heat oil in a frypan over medium heat. Add breadcrumbs and cook, stirring, for 8 minutes or until crisp. Remove from heat. Add lemon zest and freshly ground black pepper.

Place pancetta in a non-stick frypan over medium heat and cook, turning once, for 6-7 minutes or until crisp. Cool, then roughly crumble.

Add pesto to potato and toss to coat. Transfer to a shallow bowl and scatter with crispy breadcrumbs, pancetta and watercress to serve.

L-R: Broad bean & feta dip (P 198)

Beetroot & orange dip with rose and pistachios (P 198)

Hummus with spicy chorizo and green chilli (P 199)

Zucchini tzatziki with chilli, garlic and herbs (P 199)

Genius extras
Party dips

PARTY DIPS

Make these beautiful bowls ahead of time and simply serve with grissini, flatbread or corn chips.

Broad bean & feta dip

Serves 6

500g frozen podded broad beans, blanched, skins removed
2 tbs tahini
400g can cannellini beans, rinsed, drained
2 garlic cloves, crushed
Juice of 1½ lemons
200g feta
Extra virgin olive oil, dukkah and micro herbs (optional), to serve

Place broad beans, tahini, cannellini beans, garlic and lemon juice in a food processor and whiz until smooth. Add feta, season and whiz to combine.

Transfer dip to a bowl, drizzle with a thin layer of oil, cover and chill for up to 3 days, or drizzle with oil and scatter with dukkah and micro herbs, if using, to serve.

Beetroot & orange dip with rose and pistachios

Serves 6

400g can cannellini beans, rinsed, drained
250g cooked beetroot, chopped
Juice of 1 lemon
1 tsp ground coriander
2 tsp baharat (Middle Eastern spice blend – from gourmet food shops)
½ tsp dried chilli flakes
2 tbs extra virgin olive oil
1½ tbs tahini
½ tsp finely grated orange zest
Toasted pistachios and edible rose petals (optional – from gourmet food shops), to serve

Place beans in a food processor and whiz until finely chopped. Add beetroot and whiz until smooth. Add lemon, spices, oil, tahini and orange zest. Season and whiz to combine.

Transfer dip to a bowl, cover and chill for up to 3 days, or scatter with pistachios and rose petals, if using, to serve.

Hummus with spicy chorizo and green chilli

Serves 6

2 long green chillies,
  finely chopped
Tabasco Green Pepper Sauce,
  to taste
Juice of 3 lemons
400g can chickpeas,
  rinsed, drained
½ cup (140g) tahini
1 garlic clove, crushed
2 fresh chorizo sausages, casings
  removed, finely chopped
1 tbs pomegranate molasses
  (from delis and Middle Eastern
  food shops)

To make the relish, combine chilli, Tabasco and the juice of 1 lemon in a bowl. Season and set aside.

Place the chickpeas in a food processor and whiz until finely chopped. Add tahini and remaining juice from 2 lemons and whiz to combine. With the motor running, slowly add 100ml iced water in a thin, steady stream. Whiz until very smooth. Add garlic and whiz to combine. Season with salt. Transfer dip to a bowl, cover and chill for up to 3 days.

Place chorizo in a non-stick frypan over medium heat. Cook, stirring, for 6-7 minutes or until crisp. Stir in molasses and remove from heat.

Top hummus with chorizo mixture and scatter with relish to serve.

Zucchini tzatziki with chilli, garlic and herbs

Serves 6
Begin this recipe 1 day ahead.

500g thick Greek-style yoghurt
2 zucchini, coarsely grated,
  excess moisture squeezed out
1 garlic clove, crushed
Finely grated zest and
  juice of 1 lemon
2 tbs extra virgin olive oil,
  plus extra to serve
2 small red chillies, thinly sliced
Finely chopped chives and
  flat-leaf parsley leaves, to serve

Line a fine sieve with a large square of muslin or a clean Chux cloth. Set sieve over a bowl and add yoghurt. Fold over cloth to cover and place a plate on top to weigh it down. Chill overnight for the liquid to drain.

The next day, combine strained yoghurt, zucchini, garlic, and lemon zest and juice in a bowl. Season. Cover and chill for up to 3 days

Heat oil in a small frypan over medium heat. Add chilli and cook, shaking the pan, for 2-3 minutes or until crisp. Remove with a slotted spoon and drain on paper towel.

Scatter tzatziki with fried chilli, chive and parsley. Drizzle with extra oil and serve.

Chapter Eight

Bowl & spoon desserts

Hot puddings, impressive cakes and chilled desserts get a contemporary twist with clever flavour makeovers, but no fancy equipment required. Whether chocolate is your thing, you can't go past a caramel slice or you prefer a bubbling crumble, if you have a whisk, a bowl and a wooden spoon, you're set.

Lemon & coconut delicious puddings

The Australian family favourite gets a tropical twist thanks to creamy coconut milk.

Serves *4-6*

80g unsalted butter, chopped, softened
1 cup (220g) caster sugar
4 eggs, separated
Finely grated zest and juice of 2 lemons
2/3 cup (100g) self-raising flour
1 cup (250ml) coconut milk
Icing sugar and double cream, to serve

Preheat the oven to 160°C. Grease 4 x 300ml baking dishes or a 1.2L baking dish. Place butter, 150g sugar and egg yolks in a bowl and whisk for 5 minutes or until thick and pale.

Add lemon zest and juice, and whisk to combine (the mixture will appear curdled). Fold in flour and coconut milk in 2 alternate batches until completely combined.

In a separate bowl, whisk the eggwhites with a pinch of salt and remaining 70g sugar until stiff peaks form. Fold one-quarter eggwhite mixture into the lemon batter to loosen, then fold in remaining eggwhite mixture. Divide among prepared dishes, then arrange dishes in a large roasting pan. Pour in enough boiling water to come halfway up the sides of the dishes. Bake for 25-30 minutes for individual puddings or 45 minutes for 1 pudding, or until risen and just firm to touch.

Dust puddings with icing sugar and serve with cream.

Strawberry, rosemary & vodka tiramisu

This new take on the Italian classic skips the heavier coffee, chocolate and Marsala for a fresh and herbaceous tiramisu.

Serves *8*

Begin this recipe 1 day ahead.

750g strawberries, hulled
3 tsp rosemary leaves
1½ cups (330g) caster sugar
2 vanilla beans, split,
   seeds scraped
1¼ cups (310ml) vodka
3 cups (750g) mascarpone
2½ cups (600g) creme fraiche
4 egg yolks
350g savoiardi biscuits

Crystallised rosemary
2 rosemary sprigs
   (with flowers, if available)
1 eggwhite, lightly beaten
2 tbs caster sugar

For the crystallised rosemary, place rosemary sprigs on a wire rack. Brush with eggwhite and scatter with sugar. Set aside overnight to dry out.

Place 250g strawberries in a bowl. Slice remaining 500g strawberries and place in a separate bowl with rosemary leaves.

Place 1 cup (220g) sugar, 1 vanilla pod and seeds, and 1 cup (250ml) water in a saucepan over medium heat and stir until sugar dissolves. Simmer for 6 minutes or until thickened. Stir in 1 cup (250ml) vodka.

Drizzle 1½ cups (375ml) vodka syrup over sliced strawberries, and remaining syrup over hulled strawberries. Set aside for 10 minutes to macerate. Remove mascarpone and creme fraiche from the fridge.

Place egg yolks, remaining ½ cup (110g) sugar and ¼ cup (60ml) vodka, and vanilla seeds in a heatproof bowl. Whisk to combine, then place over a saucepan of gently simmering water (don't let the bowl touch the water) and whisk for 5 minutes or until thick and pale. Cool to room temperature, then add mascarpone and creme fraiche, and whisk until thick and combined.

Crumble half the biscuits in a serving dish and arrange sliced strawberries over the top. Drizzle with 1 cup (250ml) syrup. Crumble remaining biscuits over strawberries and drizzle with remaining syrup. Dollop with mascarpone mixture and use a palette knife to spread. Chill for 2 hours before serving.

Just before serving, spoon over hulled strawberries, reserving syrup. Scatter with crystallised rosemary leaves and drizzle with reserved syrup to serve.

Texas chocolate sheet cake with sour cream frosting (P 208)

Tiramisu torta caprese (P 209)

Texas chocolate sheet cake with sour cream frosting

This method of baking is known as reverse creaming, where the dry ingredients are mixed together first, then the fats are incorporated to ensure a moist, luscious crumb.

Serves *15*

125g milk chocolate, chopped
½ cup (50g) cocoa powder, sifted
175g dark (70%) chocolate, chopped
3 eggs, lightly beaten
250g sour cream
1 tsp vanilla extract
½ cup (125ml) sunflower oil
1 tsp ground cinnamon
2⅓ cups (350g) self-raising flour
1 cup (250g) firmly packed brown sugar
1 cup (220g) caster sugar
200g unsalted butter, chopped, softened

Sour cream frosting
250g unsalted butter, chopped, softened
2⅔ cups (320g) pure icing sugar, sifted
1 tsp vanilla extract
¾ cup (75g) cocoa powder, sifted
125g sour cream, at room temperature

Preheat the oven to 160°C. Grease a 22cm x 32cm x 5cm-deep baking pan and line with baking paper, leaving some overhanging.

Place milk chocolate, cocoa powder and 125g dark chocolate in a heatproof bowl with ¾ cup (180ml) water. Place over a saucepan of gently simmering water (don't let the bowl touch the water) and stir until melted and smooth. Cool to room temperature, then whisk in egg, sour cream and vanilla. Stir in oil.

Place cinnamon, flour and sugars in a bowl. Using your fingers, rub in butter until it resembles fine crumbs. Add chocolate mixture and beat to combine. Pour into prepared pan and smooth the surface. Bake for 55-60 minutes or until a skewer inserted in the centre comes out clean. Set aside in the pan to cool completely.

Meanwhile, to make the chocolate shards, melt remaining 50g dark chocolate and thinly spread over a large piece of baking paper. Cover with another piece of baking paper and roll up to form a 2cm-diameter cylinder. Freeze for 30 minutes, then unroll (the chocolate will break into shards).

For the frosting, beat butter and icing sugar in a bowl until thick and pale. Stir in vanilla and cocoa powder, then fold in sour cream. Spread thickly over cake and scatter with chocolate shards. Cut into slices and serve.

Tiramisu torta caprese

A fudgy flourless cake born in the 1920s in Capri, legend has it that the flour was left out by mistake. Add the flavours of tiramisu to combine two favourite Italian desserts.

Serves *10*

250g unsalted butter, chopped
200g dark (70%) chocolate, chopped
1⅓ cups (295g) caster sugar
5 eggs, separated
3 cups (300g) hazelnut meal
⅓ cup (35g) cocoa powder
⅓ cup (80ml) espresso
⅓ cup (80ml) Kahlua or coffee liqueur
1 cup (250ml) thickened cream
½ cup (60g) pure icing sugar, sifted
1 cup (250g) mascarpone

Kahlua syrup
½ cup (125ml) Kahlua or coffee liqueur
½ cup (110g) caster sugar

Preheat the oven to 180°C. Grease a 24cm loose-based round cake pan and line with baking paper. Place butter and chocolate in a bowl set over a saucepan of gently simmering water (don't let the bowl touch the water) and stir until melted and smooth. Cool, then whisk in caster sugar and egg yolks. Fold in hazelnut meal, cocoa powder, espresso and Kahlua.

In a separate bowl, whisk eggwhites to soft peaks, then fold into chocolate mixture. Spread into prepared pan and smooth the surface with the back of a spoon. Bake for 1 hour or until just firm to touch and the surface is beginning to crack. Set aside in the pan to cool completely, then chill for 1 hour.

Meanwhile, for the syrup, place Kahlua and sugar in a small saucepan with ½ cup (125ml) water and stir until sugar dissolves. Place over medium heat and bring to a simmer, then simmer rapidly for 6-8 minutes or until slightly thickened. Set aside to cool completely (the syrup will thicken further as it cools).

Place cream, icing sugar and mascarpone in a bowl and whisk until thick and smooth. Spread thickly over cake and drizzle with Kahlua syrup just before serving.

Salted butter, honey & pear cake

An irresistible combination of salty and sweet, this simple buttery cake is equally good with apples, if you have them on hand.

Serves *8*

250g salted butter, melted, cooled,
  plus 1 tbs extra melted butter
200ml runny honey
150g brown sugar
3 eggs, lightly beaten
½ cup (125ml) milk
2 tsp vanilla extract
2⅔ cups (400g) self-raising flour
1½ tsp ground cinnamon
2 pears, 1 coarsely grated,
  1 thinly sliced
Juice of ½ a lemon

Preheat the oven to 160°C. Grease a 22cm round cake pan and line with baking paper. Place butter, ½ cup (125ml) honey and sugar in a bowl and stir to combine. Add egg, milk and vanilla, and stir to combine. Fold in flour, cinnamon and grated pear. Spread into prepared pan.

Place sliced pear in a bowl with lemon juice and 2 tbs honey, and gently toss to combine. Arrange over batter in a fan pattern. Bake for 1 hour 40 minutes or until a skewer inserted in the centre comes out clean. Brush with extra butter and remaining 35ml honey, and scatter with ¼ tsp salt flakes to serve.

Caramel honeycomb layer cake (P 214)

Lemon & raspberry Eton mess cake (P 215)

Caramel honeycomb layer cake

This lush caramel cake is finished with golden syrup frosting, crushed shortbread and honeycomb as a nod to the Golden Gaytime, a classic Australian ice cream.

Serves *10*

150g unsalted butter, chopped, softened
200g brown sugar
½ cup (110g) caster sugar
4 eggs, separated, at room temperature
450g jar dulce de leche (a thick caramel made from condensed milk – from gourmet food shops)
2 tsp vanilla bean paste
250g sour cream, at room temperature
3 cups (450g) self-raising flour, sifted
100g shortbread, crushed
2 x 50g chocolate honeycomb bars, crushed

Golden syrup frosting
375g unsalted butter, chopped, softened
3 cups (360g) pure icing sugar, sifted
1 vanilla bean, split, seeds scraped
½ cup (125ml) golden syrup

Preheat the oven to 170°C. Grease 2 x 20cm round cake pans and line with baking paper. Whisk butter, sugars and egg yolks in a bowl until thick and pale. Add eggwhites, dulce de leche and vanilla, and whisk until smooth. Add sour cream and whisk well. Fold in flour. Divide mixture between prepared pans and bake for 55 minutes or until a skewer inserted in the centre comes out clean. Set aside in the pans to cool completely.

When cool, use a serrated bread knife to trim the tops of the cakes to level, then slice each cake in half horizontally.

For the frosting, beat butter, icing sugar and vanilla seeds in a bowl until thick and pale. Add golden syrup and beat to combine.

Place 1 cake layer on a serving plate or cake stand and spread with ½ cup frosting. Top with another cake layer and repeat until you have 4 layers. Spread the outside of the cake with remaining frosting, then press crushed shortbread and chocolate honeycomb over the sides and top. Chill until needed or serve immediately.

Lemon & raspberry Eton mess cake

The ultimate cheat's recipe, this impressive cake makes the most of store-bought ingredients and can be assembled just before serving.

Serves *8-10*

300ml thickened cream
½ cup (60g) pure icing
    sugar, sifted
1 tsp vanilla bean paste
Finely grated zest of 1 lemon,
    plus extra zest to serve
200g mascarpone
100g store-bought meringue,
    crumbled
2 x 230g store-bought round
    sponge cakes
½ cup (160g) raspberry jam,
    warmed
125g raspberries
Micro mint or small mint leaves,
    to serve

Place the cream and icing sugar
in a bowl and whisk to soft peaks.
Add the vanilla, lemon zest and
mascarpone, and whisk to firm
peaks. Fold in meringue.

Place 1 sponge on a serving plate
or cake stand and spread with half
the jam. Top with half the meringue
cream, then drizzle with remaining
jam. Top remaining sponge with
remaining meringue cream, using
a palette knife to create peaks,
then place on top of the first cake.
Scatter with raspberries, mint and
extra lemon zest to serve.

Rhubarb, apple & halva crumble

Halva, a traditional Middle Eastern sweet made from tahini, forms the base of this nutty crumble topping.

Serves *6*

1 large bunch rhubarb, trimmed, cut into 10cm pieces
3 Granny Smith apples, peeled, cored, cut into eighths
2 tsp vanilla bean paste
1 cup (220g) caster sugar
½ cup (125g) firmly packed brown sugar
2 tbs cornflour
1 tsp ground cinnamon
Vanilla ice cream or thickened cream, to serve

Halva crumble
1²/₃ cups (150g) rolled oats
200g halva (from delis or gourmet food shops), crumbled
¹/₃ cup (50g) plain flour
100g cold unsalted butter, chopped

Preheat the oven to 180°C. Place rhubarb, apple, vanilla, sugars, cornflour and cinnamon in a bowl and toss to combine. Spread in an even layer into a 30cm round baking dish. Place dish on a baking tray.

For the crumble, place oats, halva and flour in a bowl. Using your fingers, rub in butter until it resembles coarse crumbs, then roughly clump mixture together. Scatter over fruit mixture. Bake for 50 minutes or until golden and bubbling. Serve hot with ice cream or cream.

Carrot, parsnip & zucchini cake with pistachio praline

Why stop at just one vegetable when you can have three? This super-moist cake is crowned with a luscious cream cheese frosting.

Serves *8*

2⅔ cups (400g) self-raising flour
2 tsp each ground cinnamon
 and ginger
½ tsp each ground allspice
 and cloves
1 tsp freshly ground black pepper
1 cup (220g) caster sugar
¼ cup (20g) desiccated coconut
4 large eggs, lightly beaten
400ml sunflower oil
100g dried apricots,
 finely chopped
1 each zucchini, small parsnip
 and carrot (about 320g in total),
 coarsely grated

Pistachio praline
½ cup (110g) caster sugar
¼ cup (35g) pistachios,
 roughly chopped

Cream cheese frosting
400g cream cheese, softened
100g unsalted butter,
 chopped, softened
2 cups (240g) pure icing
 sugar, sifted

For the praline, line a baking tray with foil. Place sugar in a frypan over high heat, shaking until a thin, even layer. Cook, shaking the pan occasionally, for 4-5 minutes or until a golden caramel forms. Add nuts and swirl to coat, then pour onto prepared tray. Set aside for 30 minutes to set, then crush to a rough praline.

Preheat the oven to 180°C. Grease a 22cm round cake pan and line with baking paper. Sift flour and spices into a bowl with a pinch of salt. Stir in sugar and coconut. Place egg and oil in a separate bowl and whisk to combine. Stir oil mixture into dry ingredients, then fold through apricot and grated vegetables.

Spread mixture into prepared pan and bake for 1 hour 15 minutes or until a skewer inserted in the centre comes out clean. Set aside in the pan to cool completely, then use a serrated bread knife to trim the top of the cake to level.

For the frosting, place the cream cheese in a microwave-safe bowl and microwave on medium for 1 minute to warm. Remove from microwave, add butter and icing sugar, and whisk until smooth (chill mixture for 15 minutes if too loose). Spread frosting over cake. Scatter with praline to serve.

White chocolate & ginger caramel slice (P 222)

Banoffee sheet cake (P 223)

White chocolate & ginger caramel slice

Refresh your caramel slice recipe with silky white chocolate and tangy ginger.

Serves *10*

1⅓ cups (200g) plain flour
270g unsalted butter,
  melted, cooled
100g brown sugar
50g desiccated coconut
1 tbs ground ginger
1 tsp vanilla extract
3 x 395g cans sweetened
  condensed milk
½ cup (125ml) golden syrup
300g white chocolate, chopped
3 tsp vegetable oil

Preheat the oven to 170°C. Grease a 20cm x 30cm lamington pan and line with baking paper. Place flour, 150g butter, sugar, coconut, ginger and vanilla in a bowl and stir to combine. Press into the base of the prepared pan. Bake for 25 minutes or until golden. Set aside to cool.

Place condensed milk, golden syrup and remaining 120g butter in a saucepan over medium-low heat and stir until smooth. Pour over base and bake for 30-35 minutes or until dark golden. Set aside to cool completely.

Place chocolate and oil in a bowl set over a saucepan of gently simmering water (don't let the bowl touch the water). Allow to stand for 5 minutes, then stir until melted and smooth. Cool slightly, then pour over caramel. Chill for 2 hours or until set.

Remove from fridge and cut into slices to serve.

Banoffee
sheet cake

Everyone loves a great banana cake and everyone loves banoffee. So smother your next creation with decadent dulce de leche and cream for an impressive yet effortless tray cake.

Serves *10*

2²/₃ cups (400g) self-raising flour
½ cup (110g) caster sugar
1 cup (250g) firmly packed
  brown sugar
250g unsalted butter,
  chopped, softened
4 eggs, lightly beaten
2 very ripe bananas, mashed
250g sour cream
2 tsp vanilla bean paste
300ml double cream,
  whisked to stiff peaks
450g jar dulce de leche (a thick
  caramel made from condensed
  milk – from gourmet food shops)

Preheat the oven to 160°C. Grease a 20cm x 30cm x 5cm-deep baking dish and line with baking paper. Place flour and sugars in a bowl with a pinch of salt. Add butter and toss to coat. Using your fingers, rub in butter until it resembles fine crumbs. Fold in egg, banana, sour cream and vanilla until a smooth batter. Spread into prepared pan and bake for 45-55 minutes or until a skewer inserted in the centre comes out clean. Set aside in the pan to cool completely.

Place cream in a bowl and gently fold through dulce de leche. Spread thickly over cake using a palette knife. Cut into pieces and serve.

Ricotta, cinnamon & plum skillet cake

Somewhere between a baked ricotta and a cheesecake, this creamy skillet cake makes the most of in-season stone fruit. Change it up with peaches, nectarines or apricots.

Serves *8-10*

1 cup (250ml) maple syrup
2 vanilla beans, split, seeds scraped
150g unsalted butter,
  melted, cooled
1 tsp ground cinnamon
6 plums, halved, stones removed
350g shortbread, crushed
1²/₃ cups (400g) fresh ricotta
¼ cup (60ml) pure (thin) cream
2 eggs, lightly beaten

Preheat the oven to 180°C. Place ½ cup (125ml) maple syrup, 1 vanilla pod and seeds, 50g butter and cinnamon in a 24cm x 5cm-deep ovenproof skillet over medium heat, swirling until butter has melted. Add plum halves, cut-side down, and cook for 5 minutes or until glazed and softened. Transfer to a tray, drizzle with cooking liquid and set aside. Wipe out skillet.

Place shortbread and remaining 100g butter in the skillet and stir to coat. Press into the base and sides of skillet. Bake for 15 minutes or until golden. Set aside to cool.

Meanwhile, place ricotta, cream, egg, and remaining ½ cup (125ml) maple syrup and vanilla seeds in a bowl and whisk to combine. Pour over cooled base and press plum halves into the top. Bake for 50 minutes or until the edges are firm but the centre still has a slight wobble. Cool to room temperature, then chill for 2 hours or until cold.

Cut into wedges to serve.

Fig, maple & brown butter trifle

Browning the butter is the ultimate addition to the rich mascarpone cream layer, adding nutty flavour to this celebration centrepiece.

Serves *10*
Begin this recipe at least 4 hours ahead.

3 titanium-strength gelatine leaves
1 cup (250ml) maple syrup
125g unsalted butter, chopped
600ml thickened cream
1 cup (120g) pure icing sugar, sifted
2 tsp vanilla bean paste
1kg (4 cups) mascarpone
½ cup (125ml) Cointreau
  or orange liqueur
200g ginger biscuits, crushed
6 figs, halved

Cointreau & maple syrup
½ cup (125ml) maple syrup
½ cup (125ml) Cointreau
  or orange liqueur

For the syrup, combine the maple syrup and Cointreau in a bowl and set aside.

Soak gelatine in cold water for 5 minutes to soften. Squeeze excess water from gelatine, then place in a heatproof bowl with 1½ cups (375ml) boiling water and stir to dissolve. Stir in the maple syrup, then pour into a trifle dish. Chill for 4 hours or until set.

Meanwhile, to make the brown butter cream, melt butter in a saucepan over medium heat. Cook, shaking the pan occasionally, for 5 minutes or until a light nutty brown. Remove from heat and set aside to cool to room temperature.

Whisk 300ml cream, icing sugar and vanilla to soft peaks. Add mascarpone and whisk until thick and smooth. Add cooled brown butter and whisk to combine (the mixture may look slightly curdled, but the addition of more cream will smooth out the texture). Gradually add Cointreau and remaining 300ml cream, and carefully whisk until thick but not stiff peaks.

Spoon half the brown butter cream over jelly, then top with crushed biscuit. Spoon over remaining brown butter cream. Arrange figs over trifle. Refrigerate until needed or drizzle with syrup and serve immediately.

L-R: Strawberry & coconut ice cream (P 230)
Peaches & cream ice cream (P 230)
Blackberry & lemonade sorbet (P 230)
Tutti frutti ice cream (P 231)
Choc-banana vegan ice cream (P 231)

Genius extras
Ice cream & sorbet

ICE CREAM & SORBET

*Make ice cream and sorbet
at home with no need for
an ice cream machine.*

Strawberry &
coconut ice cream

Makes *1.2L*
Begin this recipe 1 day ahead.

250g strawberries, hulled
1 cup (250ml) runny honey
1kg coconut yoghurt

To make the strawberry puree,
place strawberries in a blender with
70ml honey and ¼ cup (60ml) water
and whiz until smooth. Strain
mixture through a fine sieve into
a saucepan and place over medium
heat. Bring to a simmer and cook
for 10 minutes or until reduced by
half. Transfer to a bowl and chill.
   Meanwhile, combine yoghurt
and remaining ¾ cup (180ml) honey
in a bowl and transfer to a 1.2L
container. Drizzle with chilled
strawberry puree and use a spoon
to swirl into yoghurt mixture.
Freeze overnight or until firm.

Peaches & cream
ice cream

Makes *1.5L*
Begin this recipe 1 day ahead.

400g drained canned peaches
1 tbs vanilla extract
600ml thickened cream
1 cup (250g) mascarpone
½ cup (110g) caster sugar
395g can sweetened
   condensed milk

Place peaches and vanilla in a food
processor and whiz until smooth.
Set aside ¼ cup (60ml) peach
puree. Transfer remaining puree
to a stand mixer fitted with the
whisk attachment. Add remaining
ingredients and whisk on medium
until thick and combined. Transfer
to a 1.5L (6-cup) container. Drizzle
with reserved peach puree and use
a spoon to swirl into cream mixture.
Freeze overnight or until firm.

Blackberry &
lemonade sorbet

Makes *1L*
Begin this recipe 1 day ahead.

550g frozen blackberries
1 eggwhite
1 tbs vanilla bean paste
2 cups (500ml) lemonade

Place all ingredients in a blender
and whiz until smooth. Transfer
to a 1L (4-cup) container and freeze
overnight or until firm.

oc-banana
an ice cream

5 1L

is recipe 1 day ahead.

ripe bananas, cut
1cm pieces, frozen
acao powder
250ml) almond milk
(180ml) maple syrup
(30g) cacao nibs

anana, cacao powder,
milk and maple syrup in
processor and whiz until
Transfer to a 1L (4-cup)
er and scatter with cacao
eze overnight or until firm.

or overnight until firm.

Index

Breakfast

Banana, oat & buttermilk
  spice bread *16*
Banana, pear & sweet potato
  spelt bread *16*
BLAT quinoa bowl with tomato
  & bacon ragu *20*
Brown rice nourish bowl with
  asparagus and sauerkraut *21*
Carrot & haloumi rosti with
  cauliflower hummus *15*
Chocolate & cherry slice *33*
Coconut & pistachio rice bars *33*
Garlic & olive oil butter beans
  with smoked salmon *24*
Indian breakfast bowl with
  dill yoghurt and paneer *23*
Olive oil granola with rosemary
  & apricot jam *14*
Overnight oat & chia pancakes
  with honey-roasted grapes *28*
Pecan pie overnight oats *28*
Pina colada protein balls *36*
Prune & hazelnut brownie balls *36*
Quinoa & date caramel slice *32*
Spiced carrot cake bars *32*
Turkish delight protein balls *37*
Vanilla latte protein balls *37*
Vintage cheddar & zucchini slice *10*

Desserts & sweet things

Banana, oat & buttermilk
  spice bread *16*
Banana, pear & sweet potato
  spelt bread *16*
Banana pecan tart with bourbon
  and burnt butterscotch *71*
Banoffee sheet cake *223*
Blueberry, orange &
  gin-spiked galette *85*
Caramel honeycomb layer cake *214*
Carrot, parsnip & zucchini cake
  with pistachio praline *219*
Fig, maple & brown butter trifle *227*

Fried apple & cinnamon hand pies *81*
Ice creams & sorbets
  Blackberry & lemonade sorbet *230*
  Choc-banana vegan ice cream *231*
  Peaches & cream ice cream *230*
  Strawberry & coconut ice cream *230*
  Tutti frutti ice cream *231*
Lemon & coconut delicious
  puddings *202*
Lemon & raspberry Eton mess cake *215*
Overnight oat & chia pancakes
  with honey-roasted grapes *28*
Peach tart with caramelised
  passionfruit honey *82*
Pecan pie overnight oats *28*
Power balls
  Pina colada protein balls *36*
  Prune & hazelnut brownie balls *36*
  Turkish delight protein balls *37*
  Vanilla latte protein balls *37*
Rhubarb, apple & halva crumble *216*
Ricotta, cinnamon & plum
  skillet cake *224*
Salted butter, honey & pear cake *210*
Slices
  Chocolate & cherry slice *33*
  Coconut & pistachio rice bars *33*
  Quinoa & date caramel slice *32*
  Spiced carrot cake bars *32*
  White chocolate & ginger
    caramel slice *222*
Strawberry, rosemary
  & vodka tiramisu *205*
Texas chocolate sheet cake
  with sour cream frosting *208*
Tiramisu torta caprese *209*

Meats

Braised Chinese beef ribs with
  black vinegar and ginger *142*
Caramelised pork belly with
  sweet pea salad *134*
Charred T-bone with oyster sauce
  & mushroom butter *112*

Chickpea, bacon & chicken soup *159*
Chilli beef & sweet potato pie *80*
Chilli, tomato & chorizo ribollita *153*
Green miso with soba (rare beef) *150*
Grilled eggplant and prosciutto
  with smoked almonds *179*
Lamb shank, mozzarella
  & eggplant lasagne *140*
Maple caramel pork belly skewers *184*
Miso spaghetti bolognese *108*
No-egg carbonara with
  crispy brussels sprouts *108*
Oven-roasted meatballs
  with kale pesto *123*
Pork, sage & white wine manicotti *111*
Rosemary & spelt quiche Lorraine *74*
Silverbeet, ricotta & pancetta pie *76*
Spiced lamb cutlets with
  fattoush salad *97*
Tomato & bacon ragu *20*

Pasta & noodles

Baked gnocchi sugo finto
  (fake sauce) *57*
Dan dan noodles with prawns *106*
Fast tom yum *164*
Green miso with soba (rare beef) *150*
Green miso with soba (vegetarian) *150*
Lamb shank, mozzarella
  & eggplant lasagne *140*
Miso spaghetti bolognese *108*
No-egg carbonara with
  crispy brussels sprouts *108*
Nourishing chicken pho *158*
Pork, sage & white wine manicotti *111*
Roast chicken pasta with sage,
  oregano & almond pesto *98*
Saffron, butter & tomato spaghetti
  with burrata *43*

Pizzas & bread

Eggplant parmigiana pizza *91*
No-knead overnight pizza dough *90*
Sage, thyme & garlic bread *195*

Index

Index

Thank you

Sending a giant thanks to our extended
delicious. family for their support
with assembling this collection of
our favourite new weekly recipes.
We couldn't have done it without you!

We would also like to thank the
following friends for their assistance:

Brigitta Doyle, Kirsten Jenkins,
Nice Martin, Barbara McClenahan,
Nigel Lough, Sheldon and Hammond,
Teranova Tiles, Vic's Meat

ABC
Books

The ABC 'Wave' device is a trademark of the Australian Broadcasting Corporation
and is used under licence by HarperCollins*Publishers* Australia.

First published in Australia in 2017
by HarperCollins*Publishers* Australia Pty Limited
ABN 36 009 913 517
harpercollins.com.au

HarperCollins*Publishers*
Level 13, 201 Elizabeth Street, Sydney NSW 2000, Australia
Unit D1, 63 Apollo Drive, Rosedale, Auckland 0632, New Zealand
A 53, Sector 57, Noida, UP, India
1 London Bridge Street, London, SE1 9GF, United Kingdom
2 Bloor Street East, 20th floor, Toronto, Ontario M4W 1A8, Canada
195 Broadway, New York NY 10007, USA

National Library of Australia Cataloguing-in-Publication entry:
Title: *delicious. daily : 101+ simply brilliant twists on classic recipes*
ISBN: 978 0 7333 3865 6 (paperback)
Notes: Includes index.
Subjects: Cooking.

Editor-in-chief Kerrie McCallum
Creative Director Hayley Incoll
Food Director Phoebe Wood
Managing Editor Samantha Jones
Art Director Louise Davids
Chief Subeditor Sandra Bridekirk
Photographer Jeremy Simons
Stylist Hannah Meppem
Food preparation Lucy Busuttil, Samantha Coutts, Charlotte Binns-McDonald
ABC Books Publishing Director Brigitta Doyle
Chief Executive Officer, NewsLifeMedia Nicole Sheffield
Director of Food, NewsLifeMedia Fiona Nilsson

Cover image © Jeremy Simons
Cover and internal design by Louise Davids & Hayley Incoll
Typeset in Lyon Display, Avenir LT Std

Colour reproduction Graphic Print Group, Adelaide SA and News Life Media Premedia Production and Imaging
Printed and bound in China by RR Donnelley